TOMORROW'S
FAITH

Reviews of 'A New Framework for Christian Belief'

'This book will give much food for thought and discussion to those who want to retain their Christian faith in an age which is not drawn to traditional Church structures.'

Shirley du Boulay, author, biographer.

'There will be those who strongly disagree with the views put forward in this book, and those who feel liberated by it, as well as those who fall into a middle group. But no one can read it without being stimulated, whether positively or negatively: that I can guarantee.

Rt Revd Hugh Montefiore,
formerly Bishop of Birmingham.

'This is a book to be used rather than read. It uses acceptable language and offers an understanding of Christian faith which is contemporary and intelligible. It reinterprets traditional beliefs in the light of modern thinking, without being confrontational or strident.'

Revd Alan Horner, the Living Spirituality Network.

'The greatest benefit the book offers is to consider concepts and ideas (eg. "The Trinity") in the language of our everyday lives, largely avoiding theological terms which may act as a barrier to most of us. I greatly enjoyed reading this book and thoroughly recommend it.'

Mary Sherman, Catholic People's Weeks.

'Do not read this book unless you are ready to explore into new religious understandings. There are suggestions of how the book can be used in group study. The readership is for those with a knowledge of the Christian tradition but it is not theologically demanding.'

Leslie Cram, 'ONE for Christian Renewal'.

'I think this book is searching and brilliant and needs to be well publicised.'

Revd David Charles Edwards, Anglican

'I really wish I had read this as a "catechumen". It would have saved me a great deal of trouble!"

Gillian Paschkes-Bell, Theologian

TOMORROW'S FAITH

A new framework for Christian belief

Adrian B. Smith

BOOKS

Winchester, UK
New York, USA

Copyright © 2005 O Books
O Books is an imprint of John Hunt Publishing Ltd.,
The Bothy, Deershot Lodge, Park Lane, Ropley,
Hants, SO24 0BE, UK
office@johnhunt-publishing.com
www.O-books.net

Distribution in:

UK
Orca Book Services
orders@orcabookservices.co.uk
Tel: 01202 665432
Fax: 01202 666219 Int. code (44)

New Zealand
Peaceful Living
books@peaceful-living.co.nz
Tel: 64 7 57 18105
Fax: 64 7 57 18513

USA and Canada
NBN
custserv@nbnbooks.com
Tel: 1 800 462 6420
Fax: 1 800 338 4550

Singapore
STP
davidbuckland@tlp.com.sg
Tel: 65 6276
Fax: 65 6276 7119

Australia
Brumby Books
sales@brumbybooks.com
Tel: 61 3 9761 5535
Fax: 61 3 9761 7095

South Africa
Alternative Books
altbook@global.co.za
Tel: 27 011 792 7730
Fax: 27 011 972 7787

Text: © 2005 Adrian B. Smith

Design: Jim Weaver Design
Cover design: Krave Ltd., London

ISBN 1 905047 17 7

A CIP catalogue record for this book is available from the
British Library.

Printed in the USA by Maple-Vail Manufacturing Group

Acknowledgment

The author wishes to acknowledge and record his gratitude for the suggestions for the improvement of the original text by his many friends in CANA (Christians Awakening to a New Awareness). In fact this book grew out of our many stimulating discussions together.

Adrian B. Smith MA is a Catholic missionary priest who lectures, writes and leads courses and retreats on aspects of the emerging New Era of Consciousness and on the relevance of traditional expressions of Christian belief and Church practice, to our contemporary world. This is his fifteenth book.

Contents

Introduction

In common with all human beings, as spiritual creatures, Christians carry a set of beliefs about that Reality we name "God" which underlies existence and which is a guide through life. This we call "The Christian Faith". For some of us the seeds of this were planted in early childhood, from "our mother's knee", from Sunday School, Catechism class, and from our early experiences of the sacred in church. As we matured they were thought about, questioned and became more personal to us. For others, they came to us later in life as we sought to understand what becoming a Christian meant.

Whatever these beliefs mean to us now and however they influence our lives, we are invited by the Church to affirm universally held Christian truths in the formula of its Creeds. These formulations have a long history. They were composed for a particular purpose in a particular culture, and for many today, the manner in which these truths are stated does not ring true with our own experience. In all aspects of life – scientific, sociological, political, cultural, ethical, psychological – we no longer express an understanding of our world as our grandparents or even our parents did. Scientific knowledge, Biblical studies, and human consciousness have all evolved. Hence, there is a gap between the formulation of the ancient Creeds and the way we understand religious truths today.

Divine Truth is absolute and unchanging. It is an attribute of that ultimate Reality underpinning the Cosmos: "God". It can never be grasped, let alone expressed, in its totality by our limited human minds. So as we grapple with its ineffability we construct expressions of partial truths or beliefs. Behind each of our attempts to express divine truths, there lies an experience that neither a word nor a phrase can fully manifest. The articulation of our experience is necessarily limited by our language. Words like 'salvation', 'grace' and 'revelation' will mean different things to different people, because they refer to an elusive and mysterious experience.

If 'faith' means a commitment of oneself to a certain way of life, and not simply an intellectual assent to doctrines, then doubt and faith are more closely related than is often realised. If God is Ultimate Truth, then we need not be too frightened of asking questions.

There is one thing God requires of us during our passage on Earth and that is that we grow in love. God asks for our love, not for our knowledge. Our knowledge of and belief in matters Divine are no more than a means to an end: to enable us to be more loving. The function of 'religious language' is not that of giving objective, scientific information about reality, but of evoking an awareness of the Divine Mystery as it gives itself to us in the world and in life.

If our beliefs are to be nourishment for and enliven our way of living, they must relate to reality, to 'life', as each of us understands and experiences it today. Consequently it is a matter of integrity, not of disloyalty to the Church community, to endeavour to re-express the traditional manner of stating Christian truths. To do so is not to imply that these latter were necessarily erroneous: they were apposite for their time, and can still be profoundly meaningful for some people today, but for many they are no longer adequate because they are not in accord with our twenty-first century knowledge.

This book presents a contemporary alternative to traditional expressions of belief and is offered as an invitation to think through each statement and formulate for ourselves one that more nearly resonates with our own understanding and experience, and which will help us on our spiritual journey by leading us to a new awareness of a richness in Christian beliefs perhaps not previously perceived.

NOTE

At the head of each chapter are two expressions of Christian belief. The first expresses *A Familiar, Traditional Understanding*, while the second, headed *A Contemporary Understanding*, is a statement drawn from the writings of a variety of theologians of different Christian denominations. *The text that follows amplifies the second expression.*

Part A: The Bible and Revelation

1 Revelation

A FAMILIAR, TRADITIONAL UNDERSTANDING

- The Bible is the sole source of God's revelation.

- There are truths which we could not have known except for God's revealing them to us.

A CONTEMPORARY UNDERSTANDING

- The Universe constitutes our primary source of revelation.
- 'Revelation' is born out of human experience and can only be understood and expressed within the bounds of human experience.

Humanity has always been a seeker after Truth. To seek the truth about earthly matters is one thing and we rely on the systems of knowledge developed by the sciences and humanities to guide us. But to seek to understand God and the workings of God is quite another matter. Since God has traditionally been thought to be external to our Universe, it has been the Christian belief that only God can tell us about God and that therefore such knowledge must come from somewhere outside the known Universe, and directly from God, its creator.

The majority of Christians regard the Bible as their only source of knowledge about God because it is the inspired word of God. Certainly St Augustine (354-430) did when he wrote: 'Nothing is to be accepted except on the authority of Scripture, since greater is that authority than all powers of the human mind'.

By whatever means the truth about God comes to us, when it is expressed in the Bible, it is inevitably in the words of the writer's language and therefore suffers all the limitations, first of all of the writer putting his inspiration into human thought form and secondly of expressing those thoughts within the cultural boundary of a particular language and its vocabulary.

The veteran Catholic theologian of the Second Vatican Council (1962-1965), Professor Edward Schillebeeckx, writes:

> 'The word of God is the word of human beings who speak of God. To say, just like that, that the Bible is the word of God is simply not true... The biblical writings are human testimonies to God... The new theology cannot be understood without this concept of Revelation mediated by history, of the interpretative experience of human beings. When the mediation is not accepted, one inevitably slips into fundamentalism'.

We differ from those Muslims who believe every word in the Qur'an was dictated word for word to Mohammed who learnt it by heart and taught others who wrote it down faithfully over a period of twenty-three years. We acknowledge that our Bible – both the Hebrew Scriptures which we call the Old Testament and the New Testament – is a collection of writings, a whole library, written by many people over a period of several hundred years. This 'library' contains many different styles of literature: history, myth, metaphor, poetry, prayers, correspondence, prophecies, laws, regulations, epics, prose, parables, fables, dreams, visions.

So however knowledge of God comes to us it can only be thought about and expressed in the thoughts and words of human beings. We acquire knowledge in two ways. One source is through our five senses of sight, hearing, smell, touch and taste. In other words it comes to us from outside ourselves. If it comes to us from sight or hearing it will usually come from other people, in which case it will be second-hand knowledge. (Just think back how you first came to learn about God. Was it not what you were taught by someone else?) Our reason then analyses this knowledge and stores it away for future use. So we call this 'rational' knowledge.

The second way comes to us with a flash of enlightenment, of inspiration, from within us and we call it intuitive knowledge. But to make any sense of intuitive knowledge it has to be thought *about* and so be rationalised. The first source tells us *about* God: the second may be an experience *of* God. In either case our vision of God can come to us only out of the reality of our lives lived on this Earth.

There is no divine truth that reaches us from anywhere outside our Universe. We have to discover truth – about God and God's purpose for creation – from within creation itself. As Thomas Berry, the cultural historian and theologian, has said: 'The Universe is the primary revelation of the divine, the primary scripture, the primary locus of divine-human communion' and consequently the only source of anything we can know about God.

So today as we wonder at the vastness of the Universe with its ten billion galaxies of which our Milky Way is but one, containing ten billion suns other than our own, and on the other hand the tiniest form of life on Earth, and the beauty and intricacy of it all, we have to acknowledge that what we read in the Bible is not all there is to know about God.

Part A: The Bible and Revelation

2 The Bible

A FAMILIAR, TRADITIONAL UNDERSTANDING

- The Bible is the once-and-for-all statement of Divine Truth.

A CONTEMPORARY UNDERSTANDING

- Each age needs to reinterpret afresh the Biblical message if its underlying Truth is to be our inspiration.

The Christian Bible, made up of two parts, the Hebrew Scriptures and the New Testament, is a collection of writings that have been composed over a long period. The Hebrew Scriptures (Old Testament) were probably written over a period of a thousand years while the New Testament was probably completed around 100 CE. Scholars are not in agreement about the order in which the parts of either the Old or New Testaments were written. For instance it was only towards the end of the Chosen People's exile in Babylon, or even after their return to Palestine, that the first chapters of Genesis were written; not, as many people suppose, the first to be written because they appear at the beginning of the Bible. That the Bible is not a straight-forward book is the first factor we have to take into account.

A second is that the writers, coming from an ancient and Jewish culture, had quite a different concept of Truth from us. We read something, in the daily paper, for instance, and ask 'Is it true?', 'Did this really happen?'. We insist upon accuracy and detail in recording history. We expect what is recorded to represent objective facts. Not so those who wrote the Bible, either Old or New Testament. Their wish was to convey a spiritual truth rather than to give an accurate account of facts. We notice that although the Bible is largely about people there is hardly one description of a particular person. We don't even have a description of Jesus' physical appearance. The writers were not concerned about historical accuracy nor about dates. If they want to say someone was very old when he died they say something like: 'After the flood Noah lived for 350 years and died at the age of 950' (Gen. 9:28-29). In Exodus (12:37) we read of the number of Israelites who escaped from Egypt: 'There were about 600,000 men, not counting women and children'. If this is taken literally it would mean over a million people wandering around the desert for 40 years. Again, the number 40 (40 years in the desert, Jesus' 40 days of fasting in the desert, 40 days from the Resurrection before the coming of the Spirit at Pentecost) is not meant to be an exact number. The number 40 indicates a period of preparation. Twelve usually indicated the universality of peoples: the twelve tribes of Israel, twelve Apostles to correspond to the tribes.

A third factor to take into account is that we cannot be certain which were the original texts. The Bible used by Catholics and the Orthodox have more books in them than that used by Protestants because the latter based their collection on the Hebrew texts of the Old Testament while the former based theirs on the Greek texts. The amazing discovery in a cave near Nag Hammadi in Egypt in 1945 brought to light many texts which were in wide circulation among early Christians: Gospels attributed to Thomas and Philip, texts recording the acts of Peter and the twelve disciples, apocalypses attributed to Paul and James, and so on.

And then a fourth factor to be born in mind all the time we read our Scriptures is that the truth as experienced by each writer is diminished when it has to be expressed within the confines of a language belonging to a particular culture at a particular time in history. Truth can only be expressed partially, as truths. The culture in question is middle-eastern, Jewish. This is obviously the case regarding the Hebrew Scriptures but it applies equally to the New Testament. Jesus was a Jew, expressing himself with the thought patterns of his race, and so were the apostles and evangelists.

What conclusions are we to draw? The passages of the Bible are not, as some Christians would hold, to be understood literally. We cannot say the Books of the Bible are records of Divine Revelation, by which is meant truths which we could not know without God revealing them to us directly. Writing in *Nature, Man and God* Archbishop William Temple says:

> 'There is no such thing as revealed Truth. There are truths of revelation, that is to say, propositions which express results of correct thinking concerning revelation; but they are not themselves directly revealed'.

The books of the Bible are interpretations of a revelation, interpreted with the limitations of a human author, of his personal knowledge about the world, writing out of the background of his own belief system, within a Jewish culture at a particular moment of that people's history, writing with a special purpose in mind in a language which has since come down to us through three or four generations of translation.

There is no such thing as a timeless expression of truth. To regard the words of the Bible as conveying the same meaning for all time is to be disloyal to their message. To understand the old words literally in new circumstances is to give, not the same but a new message. Consequently, each age, each culture needs to re-interpret the message afresh if it is to be loyal to the original truth.

Part A: The Bible and Revelation

3 The Gospels

A FAMILIAR, TRADITIONAL UNDERSTANDING	A CONTEMPORARY UNDERSTANDING
• Jesus' actions and words are accurately recorded in the Gospels.	• Jesus is the person of whom the Gospels speak: a product of memory, reflection, revision and community experience.

There is nothing every Christian would wish more for than to be able to read a biography of Jesus. We expect biographies to tell us all about the person, their appearance, their personality, their strong and their weak points as well as an historical record of their lives.

But it happens that in the four gospels we have none of that. They are not, and they never were meant to be, biographical. They were not written like a diary at the time of Jesus' life. Mark's gospel was most probably the earliest of the four and was written some 35 years after the crucifixion. Luke's came next, borrowing heavily from Mark and then came Matthew who borrowed from both. John's gospel came much later, probably around the year 100. Biblical scholars think it likely that there were already some earlier texts written, but now lost, upon which the evangelists drew. It is supposed that there was one (designated 'Q', a shorthand for *Quelle* which means 'source' in German) being a collection of the sayings of Jesus. Each Gospel was written for a particular readership to give those people what the writer felt they ought to know about the 'Good News' of Jesus.

In contemporary terms we can regard the evangelists as Jesus' 'spin-doctors'. Good spin-doctors do not falsify the truth but they put a particular spin on their announcements so as to show up their hero or his policy in the best possible light in relation to a particular audience. The heart of the Good News the evangelists want us to hear is what Jesus told us about God's intention for this world which he spoke of as 'The Kingdom of God'. But even this central message is not defined and we have to build up a composite picture of it from what Jesus is reported to have taught us – mostly in parables – and how Jesus lived this vision in his own life, his own values and the miracles he performed.

Since the gospels are not accounts of what exactly happened, we can understand why we find apparent contradictions. The writers were less concerned about historical facts than about the spiritual meaning behind them.

Because the New Testament opens with the four gospels most Christians presume that they were not only written in the Matthew, Mark, Luke, John order but that they were written before all the other books that follow. This is not so. Most of the letters attributed to Paul are the earliest texts of the New Testament. This is an important point. Paul wrote letters to Christian communities that already existed, that were already attracted by the Good News of Jesus, or at least what they had heard of this Good News according to Paul's interpretation of it. (We must remember that he was not an eye-witness to the life of Jesus and that he learnt about Jesus from those that were. So Paul's message is already second-hand.)

For all the above reasons we cannot be sure that we have an accurate account of almost any of the reported words of Jesus nor of many of the events. In fact we can be sure that we have very little record of what actually occurred and what was actually said, although we may believe that something along the lines of what is reported occurred. This is why we have to admit that the gospels are a product of the memory, reflections and experiences of the early Christian communities. By the time the gospels were written, the new Jesus movement had parted from its Jewish roots and begun to structure itself into a new religion with its own form of worship. Yet it is apparent that Jesus never intended to found a new religion. He gave us no rubrics for worship, he did not ordain any priests to lead the liturgy nor give us any dogmatic definitions. All these have emerged as the new communities became more structured.

Furthermore, we must not forget that Jesus spoke his message in Aramaic, a language which is much more a reflection of an eastern than of a western way of thinking, and this has been translated into languages of quite different cultures in which lots of the nuances have been lost.

And finally, when reading the gospels we have to remember that their contents is written with the hindsight of the resurrection experience. If, like me, you get half way through reading a good murder story, then feel compelled to turn to the last chapter to learn who the villain was, your reading of the rest of the story will be tinted with this knowledge, it will be quite different. The Jesus the gospels tell of is not the Jesus whom the ordinary people met on the shores of the Lake of Galilee but the glorious Jesus as his followers liked to think of him, seen through the memory and the stories about him from other people.

Part A: The Bible and Revelation

4 Continuous Revelation

A FAMILIAR, TRADITIONAL UNDERSTANDING

- Revelation reaches its climax in Jesus.

A CONTEMPORARY UNDERSTANDING

- Revelation is ongoing. We can never possess it in its fullness.

A great deal of what has traditionally been taught in the Church about Jesus, until more recent times, has concentrated on Jesus being 'God the Son'. It has focused on his divinity rather than his humanity. The reasoning went something like this: We know that God has all perfection, Jesus is God, therefore Jesus was perfect.

But in truth we cannot start from an idea of what God is like because we do not know what God is like except from what we can learn from the Creation in which God is mirrored. Among these mirrors is the human person. Jesus was just such a mirror. He is quoted as saying: 'Whoever has seen me has seen the Father' (John 14:9). According to these words he knew that he mirrored God in as complete a way as possible for a human being. Consequently we cannot say we know about Jesus because we know about God (which we don't really) but rather that we know about God because we believe Jesus reflects the Divine. St Paul calls Jesus 'the image of the unseen God' (Col. 1:15).

Peter de Rosa, in his book *Jesus who became Christ*, wrote: 'Christ is the parable of God. He is the image, the perfect mirror, the complete model of God'. In seeing Jesus we see a three-dimensional image of a multi-dimensional God.

Christians believe that Jesus is the supreme revelation of God in the sense that such a revelation cannot be added to in subsequent history. This is why he has been given the title of the Christ. If we think of the title 'Christ' – and it is a title, not a name – as meaning the anointed one, the chosen one, then we cannot disallow that in human history there have been many very enlightened, holy people who have also been mirrors of the Divine in their lives: other Christs. St Paul wrote: 'It is no longer I who live, but it is the Christ who lives in me' (Gal.2:20) and in Colossians (1:27) he wrote: 'God's plan is to make known his secret to his people, this rich and glorious secret, which he has for all peoples. And the secret is that Christ is in you'. And elsewhere we read that 'the Church is Christ's Body' (Eph.1:23).

It is through all these Christs, these mirrors of God, that God reveals himself to us. And this includes the holy people of other religions. Christians hold that Jesus is the most complete of all the mirrors.

However, as we saw in the previous pages, we only have very limited access to actual historical facts of Jesus' words and deeds and way of life. He was a man, a Jew, living in one historical and cultural situation. For his life and his message to have any value to us today we have to re-interpret what we know in the light of total contemporary knowledge. This means we have continually to be unpacking his message to understand how it applies to our life today. This is the only way we can be true to the original. It is in this sense that revelation is on-going, never static. And nor is our knowledge about God confined to what we know of what Jesus actually said. From all around us – nature, other people, our experiences, science, our own culture – comes light to enlighten us about Jesus' message. A parable will illustrate this.

There was a small boy called Toby whose father was dying. As he lay on his death bed his father reflected on the filthy life he had led in the pursuit of happiness: drink, drugs, womanising, gambling, all of which had led instead to misery. So he called his small son to his bedside and with tears in his eyes said: 'Toby, just look at the state your Dad is in. I have led a filthy life and it has not brought me real happiness. Promise me you will not follow my example, that you will always live a clean life.' And so saying, Dad died. For the next few years, Toby made sure to wash himself thoroughly from head to foot every day. It was only when he reached the age of ten that it suddenly dawned upon him that his Dad had meant something deeper than regular washing. So here was Toby, with a new, deeper appreciation of his Dad's message. He did not receive any new information but with his maturing he understood it at a different level. So it is with us and the message of Jesus. We shall never get more information but as we mature – indeed as the Church matures as a community – we come to a new, deeper understanding of Jesus' revelation to us.

A great deal is being said these days about 'inculturation', of the way in which the Gospel message, understood in the languages and culture of the West for so many centuries, has to be re-stated to convey its meaning to cultures in the Southern Hemisphere. But inculturation is needed not just horizontally – around the world as it is today – but vertically, down through history from the past to the present. To do less is to block the truth from reaching us.

Part A: The Bible and Revelation

5 Faith

A FAMILIAR, TRADITIONAL UNDERSTANDING

- Faith is belief in doctrine.

A CONTEMPORARY UNDERSTANDING

- Faith is the framework which gives our life direction and out of which we make our judgements.

Within the Church the word 'faith' is used with three different meanings. The phrase 'The Faith' is used to mean the set of truths which are proposed for our belief: the doctrines and dogmas of the Church. So the phrase is used as an exhortation: 'Keep the Faith'.

In this sense Faith is conceived as a 'thing', a package of beliefs, a set of doctrines which have to be preserved from error. We speak of the Church maintaining the 'deposit of faith', the collection of truths which originate in the Bible and have been built upon in the long tradition of the Church as the Christian community has lived and experienced the Jesus event through the centuries with ever deeper insights. So we speak of catechists and Sunday School teachers 'handing on the Faith'. That is one meaning.

Before we come to the second meaning we need to distinguish between Truth and truths. Truth is one of the absolute values, like love and justice and peace and joy, of all of which we can experience something in our earthly life but none of them in their totality. To be able to experience them to that degree we would have to be God. So although all human beings have a propensity towards Truth, we all seek it, in fact we have to be content with knowing it partially: with truths. And truths can take on a different weight and different complexion at different times in our life according as we ourselves are ever changing. So Faith, in this first meaning, is not the entirety of divine Truth but a particular perspective on Truth, expressed as truths.

The second meaning of faith is that of an act of the will. It is my personal collection of truths that I have decided to believe in. The Church speaks of faith being a gift of God, meaning that not everyone is called to believe the truths that Christians claim to be divine revelation. Everyone is free to accept or reject the gift of faith. In this meaning my faith is different from your faith or anyone else's. We might all recite a Creed together or be able to tick off the same list of truths proposed to us, but how we understand them and how each impinges upon our way of life will be different. We have the free will to take on board those truths, those aspects of Truth, which are the most useful to us for our spiritual journey.

From this arises the third meaning. Our personal faith is the collection of truths that we believe in which provides us with a framework, a paradigm, out of which we can make sense of our existence on this planet and all the different aspects of our lives. We all need such a framework from which to know how to act, to give us a basis for our judgements, our personal set of values. So our faith is our life's orientation: that which sets our course, which gives us meaning and purpose and a reason for living. It answers the question 'What do you believe in?' as different from 'What do you believe?'.

Doctrines are always partial expressions of the Truth. Because they are relative, not absolute, and because they have been expressed in a language of a particular culture and particular age – and have usually been proposed for our belief by the Church to counter what was considered at the time to be an error – their expression needs constantly to be reviewed. To retain old formulations as if they had an eternal value and not constantly to be re-formulating them in the light of present-day knowledge, can lead to our being unfaithful to the original revelation.

Of all the world religions, Christianity alone seems to give more importance to what its adherents believe than how they live. Whether one is 'in' or 'out', belongs to a Church or not, is decided by whether or not one can subscribe to a list of doctrines. There can be historical reasons for this but it is important to remember that doctrines and beliefs are not ends in themselves but means to an end. That is to say that they are no more than a means to enable us to be more loving people. God values us for our love not for our knowledge. The purpose of belief is to give us a framework in which to grow in love. Our limited understanding of Truth is fuel for our love. We cannot love what we do not know. Our beliefs, our knowledge can give God nothing: our love is what God rejoices in. So in the end it is less important what we believe, provided what we believe works for us and helps us on our journey towards the fullness of love. So Faith can never be a burden: it must always be a freedom.

Part B: God

6 God

A FAMILIAR, TRADITIONAL UNDERSTANDING	A CONTEMPORARY UNDERSTANDING
• "We believe in one God, the Father Almighty, Creator of Heaven and Earth."	• We experience the Ground of Being as the creative, loving and wise Reality that underlies our ultimate concerns. This we name God.
• God has given us a full and final revelation of Himself, to be guarded against corruption.	• Humanity is still evolving so our perception of God is always in the process of developing.

The key words in each sentence are *experience* and *perception*. Our starting point to know anything about God can only be our personal and collective human experience. We have to start from where we are, not from where we are not. We can never know God as God, in the totality of the Godhead. In fact "God" is simply the name we give to the Ultimate Reality that cannot be named. The unknown 14th century author of *The Cloud of Unknowing* wrote:

> Even if a man is deeply versed in the understanding and knowledge of all spiritual things ever created, he can never, by such understanding come to know an uncreated spiritual thing ... which is none else than God! But by recognising the reason for the limitation of his understanding, he may. Because the thing that limits his understanding is God, himself alone.

Meister Eckhart, the German mystic of the 13th century made a distinction between God and the Godhead. 'God' is the God of human proportions: the Divinity brought down to a size we can comprehend and relate to. This is why it is true to say "We make God to our own image and likeness". We can only envisage God as a 'person' having all the best human qualities to the utmost degree. We know no other. Beyond this image is the transcendent God, the Godhead, we cannot grasp. Eckhart wrote:

> God and Godhead are as distinct as Heaven and Earth.
> Heaven stands a thousand miles above the Earth, and even so the Godhead is above God.

Hindus make the same distinction: between God manifest and God unmanifest.

Everything we human beings can possibly know about God is filtered through the human mind so we have to admit that there is no objective view of God, every perception is subjective. Even if we list 'facts' that we believe about God, and say we agree upon, these facts will have a different meaning for each of us. I cannot say my perception is right, yours is wrong. Every generation has to create the image of God that makes sense within the total knowledge it has of the Universe: its 'Universe Story', its cosmology.

Our perception of the divine will inevitably be partial and this is why different religions have a different perspective on God. None of us has the total picture, so none of us can say our religious perspective is right and all the others are wrong. We Christians can say no more than we believe we have received a revelation from God about God and this we hold to because it is the perception which makes the most sense to us. But ultimately it comes down to the question of what we choose to believe.

What is so tragic is that since their emergence only within the last 3,500 years, very recent time in human history, each major religion, while maintaining that love is its foundation has claimed to provide *the* right and therefore *the* unique path to God. It is a sobering thought that so many wars and conflicts between people in recent years have been caused by conflicting cultures seeking domination and using their religion – their ideology, their concept of God – to justify and motivate their action. But if our human limited understanding of God changes as it relates to the totality of our changing earth-bound knowledge, do we have to say that God evolves as we evolve? No, God does not evolve, not because God is static but because God just IS, always fully in the eternal NOW. It is we who are evolving in consciousness, in our understanding of our place in the historical and physical totality of creation and in our God-human relationship.

Even within Christian history we can see how the notion of God has evolved. The God of the Hebrews and of early Christianity was regarded as a God who acts. God was considered principally as a God who relates to the Chosen People. As the infant Church stretched westwards, there grew the tendency to define the faith and to systematise doctrine. Ontology (the study of God's Being) became more important than religious history (God's deeds). Reflection upon what God is in Himself became more important than reflecting upon the relationship of God to people. Knowledge of God through experience was replaced by rational knowledge and this latter has been the emphasis of western Christianity to this day.

St John Chrysostom (c.347-407), one of the Doctors of the Church, wrote:

> 'Let us invoke Him as the inexpressible God,
> incomprehensible, invisible and unknowable. Let us avow
> that He surpasses all power of human speech, that He
> eludes the grasp of every mortal intelligence, that the
> angels cannot penetrate Him, nor the Seraphim see him in
> full clarity, nor the Cherubim fully understand Him. For He
> is invisible to the Principalities and Powers, the virtues of
> all creatures without exception, only the Son and the Holy
> Spirit know Him'.

Part B: God

7 Holy Trinity

A FAMILIAR, TRADITIONAL UNDERSTANDING

- The Holy Trinity is defined as "Three Persons (Father, Son and Holy Spirit) in one God."

A CONTEMPORARY UNDERSTANDING

- The relational nature of God can be understood in many different ways.

Belief in the Trinity is the highest affirmation of our Christian faith. Yet many Christians are surprised to learn that the word *Trinity* appears nowhere in the Bible! It is a theological 'definition' of the Godhead which is the product of the Greek mind in the early centuries of the Church expressing analytically what is found expressed holistically in Scripture. Jesus never mentioned the word 'Trinity' but from the way he spoke about God it became apparent that he was aware of a diversity in God's unity.

Although this belief is at the very heart of Christianity it took hundreds of years for the doctrine to be formulated. As one theologian has said, the doctrine of the Trinity is simply the attempt to formulate in a comprehensible language what God has revealed in the experience of some people who knew Jesus and recognised the mystery of God in him, of people who experienced the power and life of the Spirit of Christ after the Resurrection. Its formulation, as 'three persons in one God', however, was not developed until the decades immediately following the Church Council of Nicaea in CE 325 at which Jesus was declared to be 'God the Son'.

Even to use the word 'person' of God is to employ an analogy because the only kind of person we know is the human person. In fact such a 'definition' of the mystery of God has even less meaning now than it had at the time of the Council of Nicaea. At that time the Latin word 'persona' meant the mask that people held in front of their faces to depict their role during a theatrical performance. With the development of the science of psychology today the word 'person' has a much richer content. The value of the word has changed. So to understand what the Church meant by its arid definition we need to go back to that earlier meaning. Otherwise it appears only as a dry theological-mathematical formula, hardly designed to enable us to draw closer to the God who is at the centre of our being, living out His diversity-in-unity within us.

Today theologians are proposing other expressions to give a contemporary meaning to our belief in a triune God. For example, thinking of God as Being (not as 'a' being nor even as 'the' being). John Macquarrie proposes 'movements' or 'modes' of Being. The Father may be thought of as 'primordial' Being, the Son as 'expressive' Being, the Spirit as 'unitive' Being.

Others propose that the Biblical Father, Son and Spirit can be understood as different modes of God's action – Knowing, Serving and Loving – or as three distinguishable ways in which the one God is experienced as acting in relation to us: as Creator, as Redeemer, as Inspirer. Or again, God the Father is the Ultimate Reality to which we are drawn, Jesus is the example of what we are called to become and the Spirit is the energy that enables our becoming. What is common to all these expressions is that in the Godhead there is both unity and diversity. God is relationship as well as consciousness.

In our patriachical society it was inevitable that the symbol of the Trinity should be a triangle or pyramid with the Father on top. How much more meaningful if it had been a circle to symbolise that the very essence of God as triune is relatedness.

The concept of God as Trinity is unique to Christianity among the three monotheistic religions issuing from 'our father Abraham'. In fact the very idea that there might be three aspects of God is anathema to both Jews and Muslims. Yet curiously in Hinduism we find a similar expression of a trinity of deities: Brahman (the power which sustains everything), Shiva (the deity of both good and evil, the creator and destroyer) and Vishnu (the playful god who shows himself to humanity in different incarnations or avatars, the best known being Krishna). In Hinduism there is also an understanding of creative energy as pure knowledge, pure consciousness, which develops in a tripartite dynamic of the Knower (Rishi), the act of knowing (Devata) and the object Known (Chhandas). This is not dissimilar to the model favoured by St Augustine: The Father is the Knower, the Son is the Known and the Spirit is the relationship between them: the bliss of knowing. Or we can say that since we understand God as Love, in God there is another tripartite dynamic: a Lover (the Father), the act of loving (the Spirit) and the Beloved (the Son).

Another understanding of the Trinity symbolises the three elements in God's relationship with all things in creation, namely, God, Creation and the Love which flows between them. This is sometimes expressed as Source, Manifestation and Presence.

Cardinal John Henry Newman wrote (in *The Grammar of Assent,* 1870):

> Is the doctrine of the Trinity the elaborate, subtle,
> triumphant exhibition of a truth divinely revealed
> – completely developed and happily adjusted and accurately
> balanced on its centre and impregnable on every side ...
> or does it come to the unlearned, the young, the busy and
> the afflicted as a fact which is to arrest them, penetrate
> them and support them and animate them in their passage
> through life?

The really important thing is the experience and not the formulation: no formulation can ever replace the lived experience.

Part B: God

8 Creation

A FAMILIAR, TRADITIONAL UNDERSTANDING	A CONTEMPORARY UNDERSTANDING
• God is the all-powerful, all-knowing Lord of all Creation.	• God is the Divine presence in and creative energy of the Universe.
• Creation was an act of God done once and for all at the beginning of time.	• Creation is the continuing action of God holding all things in existence.

It is instructive to look at the titles or personifications we use in our public prayers – and perhaps in our personal prayer – to address God. We call or refer to God as Lord, Judge, King, Almighty, Creator. These titles have their origin in the Hebrew Scriptures. Jewish society was a hierarchical, patriarchical society in which the male dominated and male characteristics of power, domination and control were predominant.

We see this evident in the first chapter of Genesis where the statements about creation were written in the light of the contemporary situation, probably as late as during or shortly after the Exile (or Babylonian Captivity as it is sometimes called) around 597-538 BCE. There we read such phrases as *they will have power over the fish, birds*, etc and *your descendants will live all over the earth and bring it under their control*. Titles of power for God continued into Christian worship, echoing the titles of Emperor worship of the time.

It is logical that in that paradigm God should be considered to be a male, whereas in earlier times, among our own 'pagan' ancestors, for instance, the power of creation was considered to be a feminine attribute and the creator was the Goddess. In Scripture we also find other titles of God which relate to the deepest dimensions of our lives, such as Wisdom, Truth, Love, Life.

The very word *God* is problematic. The word with which we name Ultimate Reality in English stems from a German root meaning 'good' as opposed to 'evil'. Therein lies the seed of a dualism which has probably had a profound if unconscious effect on Western religious thinking. Whereas if we turn to the Middle East where our Judeo-Christian religion originated we find names like *Elat* (Old Canaanite), *Elohim* (Hebrew), *Alaha* (Aramaic) and *Allah* (Arabic) which stem from roots more correctly translated as Oneness, the All, Divine Unity or the Being of the Universe.

Creation is not the same as manufacturing. When we make something it is always with or out of some 'material' that already exists and so it continues to exist in some form or other when we have finished making it. We can walk away from it. God is understood as the originator of the Universe in the sense that He brought it into being from nothing: no-thing. There was no pre-existence of anything. Even when we say God created the Universe 'out of nothing' our imagination plays tricks and we picture God with a lump of 'nothing'! In the Second Book of Maccabees (7:28) we read:

> I implore you, my child, observe heaven and earth, consider all that is in them, and acknowledge that God made them out of what did not exist, and that mankind comes into being in the same way.

Scientists call this first measurable moment of our existence the Big Bang. They can offer us theories about *what* happened at the beginning of time – indeed when time came into being – and *when* that was and can speculate as to *how* it happened. But they cannot tell us *why* it happened. That is a question for religion, not science. It would be helpful if scientists did not use the word 'creation' at all but spoke of the 'origin' of the Universe. 'Creation' is a religious, not a scientific, word. Creation is not an act of God done once and for all, but the eternal action by which God continues to hold everything in existence from moment to moment. Saints have called all creation 'a thought in the mind of God'.

This is why many people are finding it helpful to think of God, not as outside, apart from His creation, but as the ever-present creative energy of and within the Universe. So we discover God, encounter God in our relationship with our world, its people, its things, its events.

St Augustine (5th C) said the world was created 'with time and not in time'. There was no 'before' creation: 'before' is a time word. So we cannot speak of God existing before creation. God simply IS. God exists in an eternal NOW, at the centre of time. We have a sense of time flowing from a past to a future. But in fact the NOW moment is the only reality, we can only live in the present. What is past is no more than a memory, be it a memory preserved in books, in recordings, on film, in buildings. But we remember it, recognise it, let it influence us only in the present. The future is no more than a speculation, a possible projection.

Think of a wheel to illustrate this. We feel time moving as if we were on the rim of a rotating wheel. Like spokes, we are always at the same distance from the hub which represents God. To the eye the hub also seems to be rotating, but mathematically the very centre is a still point. Without the still point at the centre, the wheel cannot turn. T.S.Eliot spoke of 'the still point of the turning world'. God is that still point.

Part B: God

9 Past and Future

A FAMILIAR, TRADITIONAL UNDERSTANDING	A CONTEMPORARY UNDERSTANDING
• Our understanding of God is in the context of looking back to the Fall-Redemption story.	• Our understanding of God is in the context of the unfolding creation story.

Within the Christian tradition our perception of God is coloured by our understanding of all that is contained in the word Redemption since this is so central to Christian belief. According to what this word means to us we shall think of God as an ever-forgiving lover or an understanding Father or a justifier. Our understanding of Redemption is influenced by our understanding of what is called *The Fall* and of what is meant by *Original Sin*.

The last decades have seen two factors emerging which have caused theologians to re-think the meaning of these fundamental Christian doctrines. The first is the development of 'biblical criticism'. By this is meant the examination of biblical texts in order to discover how they are composed, by whom, in what context and culture, for what reason, and how different passages came to be edited together. This has revealed that the two (and contradictory) accounts of creation in Genesis were not written to be factual (of history, geography, biology or science) but to provide a theological reflection of 6thC BCE people pondering their origins. We notice there is no mention of a 'Fall'. This is a later theological, not a biblical term. In the Adam and Eve story sin is not mentioned. The first reference to sin is in chapter 4 of Genesis in the story of Cain's jealousy and murder of Abel.

A number of scholars today believe that in depicting the Paradise state the inspired writers of Scripture were not describing a past situation but a vision and hope of what is to come. The story of our evolution in Adam and Eve symbolism is traditionally interpreted in terms of their loss of the Garden of Eden as punishment for 'falling' rather than as a maturing and moving into a new state of consciousness. In the Eden setting of early *Homo erectus* our ancestors were living in a state of sub-consciousness, a state which was pre-personal, being incapable of self-reflective thought. Without self-reflective thought one lacks self-identity which enables one to appreciate that one has a separate existence from all people and objects around. The sub-conscious Eden state was one of primitive harmony because of this inability to differentiate self from the rest of nature. The expulsion from Eden symbolises humanity's emergence from a state of non self-reflectiveness to our present state of self-awareness: from the impersonal to the personal. The same transition has been undergone by each of us in our passage from our mother's womb to being birthed as an individual.

The second factor is presented by anthropology. The biblical idea of monogenesis (that all humanity descended from one couple) has been overtaken by the theory of polygenesis (from many couples). In tracing humanity's past the anthropologist Richard Leakey has argued that the evolution of the human species in different parts of the African continent took place between 7.5 million years ago with the appearance of *Homo erectus* (when the animal species began walking erect on two legs) and 1.5 million years ago, by which time there had been an expansion of brain and our ancestors had acquired the ability to make tools. The species then evolved further to what we call *Home sapiens*. The same evolutionary process was probably taking place over the same period in other areas of our planet. For instance some 40,000 years ago Neanderthals emerged from Europe and interbred with *Homo sapiens* coming north from Africa. They had different origins yet both were distinctly human. Both groups worked the environment with tools, buried their dead (which no animal does), had some knowledge of medicine and practised art with paints. Eventually the stronger breed prevailed and Neanderthals disappeared as a distinct species. So what we call Original Sin is no longer regarded by theologians as a particular sin committed by a particular original couple which all humanity inherits by physical generation. In fact there is no hint anywhere in Jewish Scripture (our Old Testament) of an inherited sin. Professor Herbert Haag, former President of the Catholic Biblical Association of Germany, writes:

> 'The idea that Adam's descendants are automatically sinners because of the sin of their ancestor, and that they are already sinners when they enter the world, is foreign to Holy Scripture. The idea that everyone inherits 'original guilt' was developed by Augustine (4th century) late in his life'.

It is more helpful to think of Original Sin as the situation of sinfulness that we are born *into* rather than *with*. Only a century ago Christians believed the Adam and Eve story to be historically true. Today, Darwin's theory of evolution is widely accepted – at least in the fact of evolution if not in his theory of how it came about.

The Bible's view of history is not a past- but a forward-looking view. The hopes and pronouncements of the prophets of Israel were directed towards bringing about God's kind of world. With the same line of thought we can regard the Atonement as not simply righting of past wrong but the creation of a new humanity, an action of God which empowers humanity to take another evolutionary step forward by overcoming our self-centredness – a step towards living in closer union with God.

Part B: God

10 God the Father

A FAMILIAR, TRADITIONAL UNDERSTANDING

- We think of God as Father because Jesus has revealed God to us in this image.

A CONTEMPORARY UNDERSTANDING

- We think of God as Father but this is not the ultimate revelation about God.

We are so accustomed to addressing God as 'Our Father' in the Lord's prayer that we lose sight of the tremendous shift this brought about in humanity-God relations at the time of Jesus. To the Jewish religious leaders such a way of addressing God was blasphemous. In fact the title used in Jesus' language of Aramaic was *Abba* which is not the rather formal 'Father' as we translate it in English but more close to 'Dad'. And this at a time when Jesus' compatriots reverenced God with such awe that He was never even addressed by name. At that period in Jewish history God was more remote and majestic than in previous eras. No wonder such familiarity with the Divine fuelled the charge of blasphemy with which Jesus was accused and which finally led to his execution.

The gospel of Matthew gives us an illustration of the deference paid to God at the time. Unlike the other evangelists, Matthew wrote his gospel for Jews who had joined the new sect of Judaism called 'The Way'. Consequently he wrote the Good News about Jesus in this perspective. So we find that when he is reporting the same sayings and parables of Jesus as Mark and Luke who speak of the 'Kingdom of God', Matthew puts the words 'Kingdom of Heaven' in Jesus' mouth. Much as today we would say 'Heaven knows' or 'Heaven help us' rather than 'God knows' or 'God help us'.

Jesus used the title *Abba* to convey the intimate relationship that he experienced with God. In the report of his deep sharing with his closest friends at the 'Last Supper', given by John, we find such phrases as 'I am in Abba and Abba is in me', 'Whoever loves me will obey my teaching. Abba will love him and Abba and I will come to him and live with him' and 'I and Abba are one'.

But Jesus wanted us also to have this same intimacy with God for he told us how we should pray: 'Our Father in Heaven...' This new way of relating to the Divine was entirely in keeping with Jesus' central message which he put across in terms of the 'Kingdom of God'. This phrase sums up the essence of Jesus' teaching, the core of which was to live the way God intended His world to be by recognising the presence of the Divine in other people and in the whole of creation. It was about a new way of relating. And if we are to accept to address God as 'Our Father' we have implicitly accepted to treat every other human being as our sister or brother. However we have to admit that after two thousand years we are far from nearing this ideal!

While appreciating that in the context of humanity's spiritual evolution this teaching of human-Divine intimacy was a great leap forward, the mental picture created when we address God as 'Father', while being helpful at some stage of our spiritual growth, may not be adequate as we mature. No one image of the Divine can be final or all-embracing when a human being tries to grasp the concept of God. The Lord's Prayer was only introduced into Christian liturgy in the 3rd century but because the Church has retained the concept of God as 'Our Father' in its worship ever since, we might be led to believe that this revelation – coming from Jesus as it did – was the ultimate stage of our spiritual evolution. It is not. It was simply the next stage which was appropriate two thousand years ago. The Church's teaching has frozen Jesus' words for all time and in all cultures, forgetting that he was a man of his own times and culture. It was not meant to be the ultimate nor the total expression of Godhead. The only way we can handle mysteries is by the use of models. It is as if Jesus was saying: 'I will give you a model of how to relate to God: as a child does to her/his father.'

With the development of the behavioural sciences we understand that maturity calls for us to go beyond the child-parent dependency to an adult-to-adult relationship between people. To get stuck at the level of the Father-child relationship to God can become a form of idolatry. We would be transforming what is no more than a model into a reality. It is not even a model that appeals to everyone. For someone who in their childhood suffered abuse from their father or step-father, or indeed never knew a father, this model can be a real obstacle. For some it can be more relevant to think of the maternal quality of the Godhead and address God as 'Mother'. Others might find it more helpful on their journey to human maturity to envision God as a friend – our closest friend – rather than as a father or mother.

Part C: Jesus the Christ

11 Jesus and His Message

A FAMILIAR, TRADITIONAL UNDERSTANDING	A CONTEMPORARY UNDERSTANDING
• Jesus is God-made-man who came down from Heaven to save us.	• Jesus is a manifestation of God who lived among us to show and empower us to live by higher values, which he called the 'Kingdom of God'.

When Luke, in his gospel, starts to record the preaching years of Jesus, he reveals a very telling incident. The people of the town of Capernaum were delighted to find there was a healer among them and they tried to keep him there. But Jesus tells them: 'I must preach the Good News of the Kingdom of God in other towns also because that is what God sent me to do' (4:43). As we saw in chapter 4 we too readily begin our journey of discovery about Jesus with our belief that 'Jesus is the Son of God', and if our image of God is of a Father who inhabits a place called Heaven, then we conclude that Jesus was sent down from there. (More of this in the next chapter.) We get a different picture of Jesus if our starting point is not the resurrected Jesus, the Christ, but the man who appeared in the towns and villages of Galilee and whom his followers had to get to know little by little.

He became a public figure, probably in his early 30s, after an obscure life in Nazareth, so remote a village that it does not even get a mention in the Hebrew Scriptures (our Old Testament). It was after his baptism by John the Baptist, that he understood that he had a God-given mission to accomplish. What was it? 'To preach the Good News of the Kingdom of God'. Nothing here about his being sent to die on a cross or to shed his blood 'for the ransom of many' or to pay a debt to God for the salvation of the world.

He understood his life's task was to reveal God's intention, as he understood it, for humanity. Picking up a phrase from his own Scriptures, which expressed the hopes of his people to be liberated from Roman colonisation, he referred to his vision as the 'Kingdom of God'. Sadly for us in the western world who favour clarity of thought, we do not find that Jesus has anywhere left us a definition of what exactly he meant by that phrase. Nevertheless it was the core of his message: it was *the* Good News. It is the most constantly recurring theme of the first three gospels, being mentioned 104 times, 91 times on the lips of Jesus. It is the subject of almost all the parables, of which 40 tell us what the Kingdom is like and 25 speak of the fate of those who are unprepared for the Kingdom.

With no neat definition to hand we have to build up a picture and this we do from two sources. Most obviously from what Jesus is reported to have said about it, but more importantly by observing the life of Jesus and the values by which he lived. The person of Jesus is the primary message. People were attracted to him in the first place, by his personality, by the way he lived, by the way he related to people and only secondarily by what he said which was his explanation of the values which dictated his way of life. The people remarked that he spoke with authority, 'unlike the Scribes and the Pharisees' because his authority was his authenticity: he lived what he believed and in that way he gave his message flesh. He lived as a Kingdom person.

Putting together what we see of Jesus' life-style and his message we can interpret the expression 'Kingdom of God' in a number of ways. Briefly as 'the world the way God means it to be'. Or: 'the situation in which life is ordered by interior, spiritual power rather than by external human-controlled power'. Or again, 'living with the consciousness of God's all-pervading presence: that all creation is divine' and consequently this calls for a new way in which we human beings relate to one another and to the natural world.

We get a further insight from the gospel of John. While the other three evangelists have Jesus declare his message in terms of the 'Kingdom', John has him declare it in terms of 'life', the fullness of life. That, for John, is what the Kingdom is about. God's plan for humanity is that we should all attain fullness of life – the fullness of our humanity – in union with God. The word 'life' or 'eternal life' occurs in John 36 times and he recounts Jesus as saying: 'I have come in order that you might have life – life in all its fullness' (10:10). Our means to receive this life already now in its fullness is to accept Jesus and his message.

Part C: Jesus the Christ

12 Jesus' Birth

A FAMILIAR, TRADITIONAL UNDERSTANDING

- God 'sent' His Son 'down' to Earth and Jesus ascended 'up' to Heaven.

- The biblical account of Jesus' birth: that 'he came down from heaven: by the power of the Holy Spirit he became incarnate from the Virgin Mary', are literally true.

A CONTEMPORARY UNDERSTANDING

- We do not think of the Incarnation or the Ascension as physically down or up. We understand them as metaphors.

- The accounts of Jesus' birth and infancy were constructed to explain his divine nature in mythological terms.

In the western world we have certain expectations of a biography so that we tend to read such literature as the gospels with the same expectations. In chapter 3 we made the point that they are quite a different type of literature from most things we are accustomed to reading. And also that they were written years after the Jesus event in the light of the person who, at that time, the authors understood the resurrected Jesus to be.

Most biographies are written after someone has become famous. The biographers then look back to the circumstances of that person's birth and early years to see if there is any indication of why they developed as they did. Of the four 'biographies' we have of Jesus, only two refer to his birth and childhood events. Mark and John, and Paul too, did not consider that part of the life of Jesus had sufficient importance to include it in their proclaiming Jesus to be Son of God.

In our own day, Cardinal Joseph Ratzinger, Prefect of the Vatican Office for the Doctrine of the Faith (the successor of the inquisional Holy Office) wrote:

> According to the faith of the Church, the divine sonship of Jesus is not based on the circumstance that Jesus had no human father. The doctrine of Jesus' divinity would not be violated if Jesus had been the product of a normal human marriage. For the divine sonship that faith speaks of is not a biological but an ontological fact; it is not an event in time but in God's eternity.

Matthew's account contains elements to be found in folk literature: a wicked king, oriental magicians, a special star. He is not intending his readers should accept that he is relating historical events. He is writing for his fellow Jews and is putting across a theological message: Jesus is recognised by the Gentiles but not by his own people. He even bends Scriptural quotations to serve his purpose. He writes 'All this happened in order to make what the Lord had said through the prophet come true, "A virgin will conceive and have a son"' (1:22-23) whereas what the prophet Isaiah had actually said (7:14) to King Ahaz was: 'A young woman who is pregnant will have a son'.

Luke's manner of portraying Jesus was to reflect upon the Hebrew Scriptures. His account of the birth of Jesus is based upon the infancy story of Samuel (I Samuel 1-2) including Mary's *Magnificat* (Luke 1:46-55) based on Hannah's prayer at the birth of Samuel. He too is not primarily concerned with historical accuracy, as the opening words of his second chapter show:

> 'At that time the Emperor Augustus ordered a census to be taken throughout the Roman Empire. When this first census took place, Quirinius was the governor of Syria. Everyone, then, went to register himself, each to his own town.'

In fact the writ of the Roman Emperor did not apply in Palestine since that country was not under the direct rule of Rome. Besides, when Quirinius was governor King Herod, whom Matthew named as being responsible for the slaying of the 'Holy Innocents' later on, had been dead for at least eleven years. The registration, for tax purposes, would not have taken Joseph and Mary to Bethlehem since Roman taxes were based on where people lived, not on their town of tribal ancestry.

We are told nothing of Jesus' childhood years because they contain no theological message. As a boy he must have been as naughty and mischievous as all the other boys in the village. This is part of growing up in experience and responsibility. If a boy was never mischievous would he be truly human? In the only event recorded of his boyhood years (Luke 2:48-49) we find him having an altercation with his parents! On one occasion in later life he said to a Jewish leader: 'Why do you call me good? No one is good except God alone' (Luke 18:19). Among his contemporaries in the small village of Nazareth he cannot have shown any signs of being different from them, which was probably why they regarded him with such resentment when he returned to preach in Nazareth and assumed the role of a prophet:

> 'Many people were there and when they heard him they were all amazed. "Where did he get all this?" they asked. "What wisdom is this that has been given to him? How does he perform miracles? Isn't he the carpenter, the son of Mary, and the brother of James, Joseph, Judas and Simon? Aren't his sisters living here?" And so they rejected him.' (Mark 6:1-3).

Not only are the gospels a mixture of history, faith and mythical imagery but so are our Creeds. Many Christians, reciting the words Sunday after Sunday, will accept all the statements as of the same historical value. Take just one expression: 'Born of the Virgin Mary'. Although the virginal conception of Jesus is a traditional

Christian belief of some weight, (belief that Mary remained 'ever virgin' during and after giving birth was a later belief) we cannot know as an historical fact the intimate physical workings of Mary's womb. (Only Mary and Joseph could have known and with whom did they discuss it?) It cannot be proved from Matthew or Luke, the only two evangelists who tell the birth story, although they clearly believed in it themselves. The virgin birth was believed, during the Middle Ages, so deeply to be a physical fact that the Jesuit Cardinal Robert Bellarmine, Saint and Doctor of the Church, declared while Galileo was on trial: "To assert that the Earth revolves around the Sun is as erroneous as to claim that Jesus was not born of a virgin." We now know that the former statement is not erroneous but true. Where does that leave us with the second statement?

But is the virgin birth really so important? If it were, surely God would have given us much more certain information about it. As Hans Kung, the well-known German theologian says:

> 'No one can be obliged to believe in a biological fact of a virginal conception'.

Part C: Jesus the Christ

13 Jesus' Humanity

A FAMILIAR, TRADITIONAL UNDERSTANDING	A CONTEMPORARY UNDERSTANDING
• Jesus is God, a Divine Being who took on human nature. • He is fully human and fully divine.	• Jesus, in his humanity, is one who is transparent to the Divine. God was as fully present and active in Jesus as is possible in human form.
• The emphasis is on the Divinity of Jesus.	• Today's emphasis is on the humanity of Jesus and his God-consciousness.
• Jesus is worthy of unconditional worship as God.	• We worship God as revealed in Jesus and pray to God through Jesus.

Who or what is Jesus the Christ is a question theologians have been struggling with, arguing about, pronouncing upon ever since the first century – and they are still at it! Even going back to our gospels and epistles is not going to help us much to work out a theology of Jesus for our time because there is not just one orthodox doctrine of Jesus presented. There are several. For instance, for Paul and in the early chapters of the Acts of the Apostles, Jesus was a man 'raised up by God' (Acts 2:23-32). The gospels of Matthew, Mark and Luke present Jesus as a miracle-worker who receives the Spirit of God and through his obedience to God is raised up to be the Christ. In the Epistle to the Ephesians (we do not know who the author was) Jesus is presented as a glorious Cosmic Christ. In John's gospel, written much later, Jesus has become the pre-existent Word of God, a quite other-worldly figure:

'The Word made flesh'. John's concept of Jesus was quite different from that of the author of the Letter to the Hebrews: 'Like us in all things but without sin'. Though the same Jesus is recognisable in each writing, the differing points of view are not surprising because there is always a subjective content to their experience of this person.

The first thing we need to be aware of, obvious though it is, yet not clear to so many Christians, is that when we speak of 'Jesus Christ', we are not using a pair of names but a name and a title. Jesus or Joshua or Yesu was his 'given' name. 'Christ' literally means 'the Anointed One' which, as a Greek word, was used in the (Greek) New Testament to translate the Hebrew word for Messiah. So we would be more correct if in our speaking and in our prayers we said 'Jesus the Christ'.

Perhaps the most important New Testament title for Jesus is 'Son of God'. At least it is for us as we understand the expression with all the theological weight which it has gathered over the Christian centuries. But we have to realise that it did not originally have the meaning in Hebrew culture which we commonly give it in the Church. Among the Chosen People the title was given to an individual or group who was close to God, under God's protection. The Jewish nation as a whole was called God's Son (Psalm 2:7), as was a devout believer. In a special way the title belonged to the King of Israel (2 Samuel 7:14). When the title is applied to Jesus in the New Testament Letter to the Hebrews – 'You are my Son; today I have become your Father' (1:5 and 5:4-5) – it is in this same sense, as a specially chosen person. So to describe Jesus as 'Son of God' was to speak of his significance rather than to account for his origins. Jesus himself uses the expression this way when, in the Beatitudes, he declares: 'Blessed are the peacemakers: they shall be called sons of God' (Matthew 5:9). Only after the Council of Nicaea in the 4th century did the phrase take on the Trinitarian meaning we give it today in the Creed as 'only-begotten Son of God'. In fact at Nicaea, the phrase 'Son of God' was promoted to mean 'God the Son'. (This should warn us of the danger of reading back into

Scripture the theological understanding which arose at a later period or which we give it today.)

There is no evidence that Jesus taught or believed in his own divinity nor can it be proved that he proclaimed himself the Messiah. He is never reported in the Gospels as publicly proclaiming this role; it is not part of his message. (He does, however, seem to agree with other people's acknowledgement of his Messianic role in private on a couple of occasions. eg. Luke 4:41.) He never said 'I am God'. In fact several times he seems to say just the opposite (eg. Mark 10:18, 15:34, John 17:3). During the Last Supper Jesus states: 'I am going to the Father for he is greater than I' (John 14:28). Only twice do his disciples call him God ('The Word was God' and 'My Lord and my God') both in John's gospel and therefore of late date.

Peter in his speech (Acts 10) to the Roman captain Cornelius, describing the high points of the Jesus-event, distinguishes Jesus from God: 'He went everywhere doing good and healing all who were under the power of the devil, for God was with him (v.38)... God raised him from death (v.40) ... and he commanded us to preach the gospel to people and to testify that he is the one whom God has appointed judge (v.42).'

Several times in the gospels we hear of Jesus praying to God (eg. during the Last Supper: John 17) and so in official Church liturgy we follow Paul's example (Romans 16:27) and pray to God through Jesus, concluding our prayers: '...*through* Jesus Christ Our Lord.'

Part C: Jesus the Christ

14 Jesus' Actions and Words

A FAMILIAR, TRADITIONAL UNDERSTANDING

- Jesus was omniscient and omnipotent from his conception.

- Everything Jesus did and said is done and said by God. He had supernatural powers because he was God.

A CONTEMPORARY UNDERSTANDING

- Jesus was limited by his humanity. His understanding of himself, of his mission and of God, developed during his lifetime.
- Jesus acted and spoke as a human being. All his powers issued from his human potential being fully realised because he was fully aware of and lived his unity with God.

Although the Church Council of Chalcedon (5th C) defined what was to become the orthodox doctrine of the *Incarnation*, it not surprisingly became tangled up in what is really a philosophical question when trying to 'explain' a mystery. It asserted that Jesus was 'truly God and truly man' without attempting to say how such a paradox is possible. It is a neat formula but not very helpful!

From what we learn from the three Synoptic Gospels (Matthew, Mark, Luke) Jesus lacked at least some of the qualities we attribute to God. He was not all-knowing; he was not all-powerful. As regards the first, it seems that Jesus not only thought of himself as a prophet, but probably as being the last prophet. He proclaimed the imminent approach of the Day of the Lord when the Kingdom of God would be fully established on Earth. This was an expectation among the Jews of Jesus' time. So he called the people to prepare for it by repentance (Mark 1:15). 'I tell you there are some here who will not die until they have seen the Kingdom of God come with power' (Mark 9:1). And Matthew (24:34) has Jesus say something similar.

While it is generally recognised today that Jesus did not intend to launch a new religion upon the world, we may question whether he even intended to found a community (the Church) to continue his mission after his death, since he believed he was living at the end of human history. The texts in the gospels that support his founding a Church were written after a Church had already become a reality in the communities founded by Paul.

Secondly, Jesus was not all-powerful in that he was restricted by the limitations from which all human beings suffer. Would he have had the physique to climb Mount Everest, or to run a mile in less than four minutes? We see his human weakness appearing on several occasions. Besides being mistaken about the timing of the end of the world – in fact he confessed ignorance about the time (Matthew 24:36) – he was tempted in the desert, he felt abandoned by God on the cross, and on at least one recorded occasion (Mark 6:5) he was unable to perform any miracles of healing because people lacked faith in him.

Of course ingenious ways have been offered to 'explain' these texts. Did Jesus, as God, really possess omniscience and omnipotence but refrain from exercising them? (We were probably taught in our childhood something like this: 'Yes, he had to learn his lessons like any other child at his mother's knee but as God he knew it already'.) If this were so, can we claim, as the Church Councils do, that he was *fully* human?

Jesus' miracles of physical healing, his demonstration of power over nature, his bringing people back to life, were not performed to show his credentials as God, nor done to win popularity or fame – on the contrary, he sometimes insisted that news of his miracles was not spread (Mark 5:43) – but they flowed from his very person as one who was fully enlightened, fully mature as a human being and so could tap the hidden energies of the cosmos. He was a spiritual healer of the kind the Church largely stopped believing in but which, with our understanding of the holistic, we are beginning to appreciate once more. Jesus was already living as a Kingdom person the message he proclaimed.

Such 'signs' of the Kingdom, as John calls them (John 2:11), were considered 'miraculous' at the time – and even now – but are heralds of all of humanity's possibilities when we too have attained that 'fullness of life' with which Jesus said he had come to empower us. During most of its history the Church has down-played these abilities, fearing their magical dimension.

For many centuries the Christian Church has over-humanised God and over-deified Jesus. While we have projected on to God the attributes of a super human being, we have in contrast concentrated on the divine aspect of Jesus at the price of neglecting his humanness. Contemporary theologians are now restoring the balance.

As we said in a previous chapter, we cannot point to God and say Jesus is like this because he is God (drawing our inspiration from John's mystical gospel, as the great theologians of the 4th and 5th centuries did), but rather we have to point to Jesus and ask how the first Christians came to the conviction that God was acting in him in a unique way. To attempt to understand Jesus in God-terms casts doubt on how genuinely human Jesus was. Theologians today are moving from 'Christology from above' and seeking to understand Jesus 'from below': 'rising up' from the Jesus of the gospels to the Christ of faith. In other words we are less concerned with the philosophical questions of what Jesus *was*, in abstract terms of substance, nature and person, but we are looking at Jesus in terms of action: what he did and said in the context of the times and culture in which he lived, and their implication for our own times and culture.

Part C: Jesus the Christ

15 Christ, the Way

A FAMILIAR, TRADITIONAL UNDERSTANDING

- From Jesus' words: 'I am the way, the truth and the life; no one goes to the Father except by me', we understand that Christianity alone possesses the true revelation. All other religions are false or inadequate.

A CONTEMPORARY UNDERSTANDING

- The way to God is also found in other religions which have different perspectives on the One Truth. But for Christians, its manifestation in Jesus is the most accessible, powerful and inspiring.

In Victorian times missionaries set out from this country for the furthest corners of the Empire to 'convert the natives' – which was synonymous with civilising them – with the dream that one day all the world would be Christian, all people saved. In fact the gospel played a vital role in the self-justification of western imperialism. They were people of their time.

Thanks to the ease of communication between East and West, to the multi-cultural and multi-faith nature of western society today there is an increasing dialogue between the followers of the world's major religions which has enabled us to think differently. At the highest level we are witnessing unprecedented gatherings of leaders of all the main religions to discuss matters of common concern: justice, peace, population and development, ecological and world issues.

It is appreciated that we all originate from the same source, the mind of the Creator, and we are all destined for the same ultimate experience of unity with the Divine. It is accepted that all religions are explorations into and applications of the Fundamental Truth or Perennial Philosophy, as Leibniz called it. The Dalai Lama has written:

> 'Every major religion of the world has similar ideas of love, the same goal of benefiting humanity through spiritual practice, and the same effect of making their followers into better human beings.'

Where religions differ is that they offer different explanations of the cause of evil and the means to overcome it.

The Second Vatican Council declared to Catholics that the religions of the world are not mere philosophies but attempts over centuries to respond to the mysteries of the human condition:

> 'Those also can attain to everlasting salvation who through no fault of their own do not know the gospel of Christ or his Church, yet sincerely seek God and, moved by grace, strive by their deeds to do his will as it is known to them through the dictates of conscience' (LG.16).

Since, as we saw before, Truth cannot be known in its entirety in our human condition, each religion is a particular but incomplete manifestation of unmanifest Truth. No religion is complete in itself: each is a sign pointing in its own way, beyond itself, to the Divine Mystery. Each may be unique in its manner of expressing Truth but because of its incompleteness it cannot claim to be unique as *the* pointer to the way. The revelation of each is a treasure to be shared, not a private possession to be defended. Religious wars have marred our history and continue today to arise from the mistaken idea of one religion that it possesses the final revelation and is therefore superior to all others.

So what are we to make of John's reporting Jesus to have said that 'No one goes to the Father except by me' or Peter's words (Acts 4:12) 'Salvation is to be found through him [Jesus] alone; in all the world there is no one else whom God has given who can save us'? We have already seen that it was unlikely that Jesus was conscious that he was the Messiah, the saviour of the world. All the 'I am ...' sayings of Jesus (for instance: 'I am the light of the world', 'Before Abraham was born, I am') are from John's Gospel only, and John was not writing so much about the human aspect of Jesus' life but of the Christ who was incarnated in Jesus of Nazareth, who did not make claims for himself.

Reinhold Bernhardt explains (in *Christianity without Absolutes*) that since the young Christian communities were under attack from the Jewish establishment, 'the sharp statements which thus arose are to be interpreted as a reaction to a quite specific challenge and not as universally valid supra-historical judgements on the religions of the world. They cannot simply be transferred to quite different situations'.

John's quotations are of the resurrected Cosmic Christ through whom the Father speaks, rather than of the historical person, Jesus. The Catholic theologian Raimon Panikkar states that no historical name or form can be the full, final expression of the Christ. This means: 'Christ the Saviour is...not to be restricted to the merely historical figure of Jesus of Nazareth'. Christ is *the* way: Jesus is *a* way.

Part C: Jesus the Christ

16 At-one-ment

A FAMILIAR, TRADITIONAL UNDERSTANDING

- Jesus was sent down to Earth by his Father to shed his blood for the salvation of the world.

A CONTEMPORARY UNDERSTANDING

- Jesus brought about the possibility of our taking a step forward towards our becoming one with the Divine.

The eminent theologian John Macquarrie tells us in his book *Principles of Christian Theology*:

'The Church has never formulated a doctrine of atonement with the same precision with which it has tried to define the person of Christ. Instead, we find several explanatory models that have developed side by side. Even in the New Testament a considerable variety of ways of understanding the atoning work of Christ is to be found',

and we might add that these explanations come from a past and a culture foreign to us. These traditional explanations employ such terms as *Redemption, Sacrifice, Ransom, Justification, Jesus gave his life, he shed his blood, Expiation, Satisfaction, Substitution.*

That the life, death and resurrection of Jesus enabled us to establish a right relationship with God is such a fundamental Christian belief that it has never been the subject of heresy. Consequently the Church has never had the need to define dogmatically *how* Jesus accomplished it and so different explanations have been offered which made sense to people in past times. Concepts like 'paying a price [to God or to Satan?] on our behalf', or shedding blood as a human sacrifice, or redeeming us from slavery, or that a loving God would wish his son to have a torturous death, do not speak to people today.

To understand how these explanations arose we need to appreciate the shattering effect the sudden death of Jesus must have had upon his closest followers. They were stunned, not only by its brutality, but by the way it came about. One moment the crowds were clamouring to hear Jesus, to be healed in some way, they were welcoming him into Jerusalem. Their hero seemed to have reached the pinnacle of popularity. The next, there was a complete volte-face, they were screaming that he should be crucified. And it was all over within a couple of days. There is not one of us who is not desolated by the sudden and untimely death of someone close to us, especially when that person is our inspiration, the cause of our hope. We grope for meaning: either a spiritual meaning (it must be God's will) or a human meaning (may it be a lesson to others not to be so fool-hardy). So with the apostles: a spiritual meaning had to be found. They searched their Scriptures, and explanations soon appeared. But Professor Geza Vermes, in his book *The Religion of Jesus the Jew*, states quite bluntly:

> [Jesus] 'died on the cross for having done the wrong thing (caused a commotion) in the wrong place (the Temple) at the wrong time (just before Passover). Here lies the real tragedy of Jesus the Jew'.

The crucifixion was demanded by human beings, not by God. It highlights human injustice, not God's justice.

Nevertheless, in Mark's account of the Last Supper we find Jesus saying: 'This is my blood of the covenant, which is poured out for many' (14:24). But since these eucharistic words are quoted differently in different gospels we cannot know what words Jesus actually used or to what extent they arose later from the development of a eucharistic liturgy in the early Church. (Some scholars do not attribute them to Jesus at all.) Whether or not Jesus thought of his death as being the required redemptive sacrifice for all humanity, it does seem evident that he went to his death freely (John 10:18).

Theologians today are regarding the total mystery of the Jesus-event, from birth, through life (with its announcement of 'Good News'), death and resurrection to ascension as being of redemptive value: not simply the crucifixion. In the Eastern Church the Incarnation was the 'saving' action.

Describing Redemption as Atonement is a more helpful word if we understand it as 'at-one-ment'. It enables us to offer an explanation, within an evolutionary context, which speaks to people of our times. It is not backward-looking, repairing the effect of humanity's 'Fall', but forward-looking, understanding the whole Christ mystery as empowering humanity to rise to a life in closer union with God.

An analogy can help us. We human beings are always drawn to strive beyond our present attainment, physically and intellectually. (Hence the Guinness Book of Records!) But it seems to be a characteristic of human nature to require one of our species to break through the barrier of human limitation in order to empower others to follow. Captain Webb who first swam the English Channel in 1875, or Edmund Hillary the first to reach the summit of Mount Everest in 1953, or Roger Bannister, the first to run a mile in under four minutes in 1954, come to mind as barrier-breakers. They opened the way for others to follow, and even to surpass them.

Teilhard de Chardin explains the Jesus-event as moving the whole of creation dramatically forward and upward. Jesus marked a unique leap towards a higher spiritual unity. He not only marked the leap, he made it on our behalf. He was able to do this because, as the icon of God, he was the perfection of humanity, free of the inner enslavement to which we are all held captive: that false ego. He empowered us, not by injecting a new power into humanity from without but by liberating a God-given gift already present but needing someone to release it, to break through the barrier of our ego on our behalf.

Thus today we are shifting the explanation of redemption from a negative one of redemption from an evil past to a positive one of release of our inner creative power to enable us to grow to the fullness of our humanity, to become the complete persons God created us to be.

Part C: Jesus the Christ

17 Resurrection

A FAMILIAR, TRADITIONAL UNDERSTANDING

- The 'Resurrection' is the belief that Jesus rose to life on the third day after he died on the cross.

A CONTEMPORARY UNDERSTANDING

- The 'Resurrection' is the way in which Paul and the evangelists affirm that Jesus is among us in a new manner of living, in a finer, spiritual manner, thus demonstrating the power of Divine life over material limitations.

Belief in the Resurrection of Jesus is the cornerstone of Christian faith. It is precisely because Jesus the Christ overcame and passed beyond death, thus giving us a faith in a life beyond death, that gives meaning to his being our 'Saviour'. Until the time of the Maccabees in the second century before Jesus there is not the slightest hint of a belief in an after-life, even though the whole world around Israel believed it. In Jesus' own day it was a highly debatable subject between Pharisees and Sadducees, with the former believing in it and the latter not (Matthew 22:23).

So not surprisingly, there is no clear report about what actually happened on Easter Sunday morning. The reports we have contradict each other in several places. Once again, the evangelists were more concerned to write about what it meant than what actually took place.

The traditional teaching, unchallenged for well over a thousand years, is faced with a contradiction arising from what science now tells us about the Universe. If we maintain that Jesus rose from the tomb with a physical body, leaving the tomb empty, we must link this belief with a literal Ascension. But the traditional belief of what happened at the Ascension requires belief in a localised Heaven – not too far away – into which a resuscitated human body can be carried by clouds. The accounts we are given of the Ascension forty days after Easter are not intended to be literal descriptions of an historical event. They are a graphic way of expressing the full integration of Jesus' humanity – and so potentially all humanity – with the divinity of God. In any case, a three-tier concept of Heaven, Earth and Hell is no longer tenable. So we think rather of Heaven being not a place in the sky but another dimension of being.

The Bible's first narrative of the Resurrection is found in Paul's writing (I Cor.15:3-8), long before the first gospel account was written. He has no mention of an empty tomb, of the disappearance from the grave of a physical body, of a physical resurrection or of physical appearances of a Jesus who would eat fish and offer his wounds for inspection. In John's gospel the Resurrection, Ascension and the awareness of the presence of the Holy Spirit at Pentecost are all put together as an Easter event, elements of the same mystery.

When Jesus rose from the dead – or as Paul says, when he was raised by God from death (Romans 10:9) and Peter too uses the passive voice (Acts 2:32 and 10:40) – it was not to resume his earthly body as had been the case in the three reported incidents when Jesus brought dead people back to life, who had eventually to face death again later. It is as if Jesus had entered another 'wavelength', which accounts for the fact that he 'appeared' only to those people who had had faith in him during his earthly life. (The word translated as 'appeared' is the Greek word *ophthe* which is normally used, not for physical sightings, but for inner spiritual vision.)

If we take the Resurrection narrative literally as Luke presents it (24:32), we have to ask such questions as: Did Jesus appear naked to his disciples, with women among them, or do we have to include the resurrection of Jesus' garments? If his appearances were physical and not spiritual he would have appeared in the body (and clothes) that his disciples expected to see. Yet there are three occasions recorded when he was not immediately recognised by those who had been closest to him.

So what are the writers of the different accounts trying to tell us? They are speaking in metaphorical terms to explain their experience of Jesus' continued presence among them. Just as the story of the two disciples walking to Emmaus and meeting Jesus on the road, his 'opening the Scriptures to them' and finally their recognising him in the breaking of bread, was not an event of a single evening but a pictorial summary of the way in which the meaning of the Jesus-event was unfolding among the disciples. It is historical in the sense that it describes a process over time which happened in the Christian community. We have to acknowledge that there will always be an element of mystery about the Resurrection as to who 'saw' what and in what form.

We notice that Paul never argues that the Resurrection was a special miracle only for Jesus. Just the opposite: Jesus Resurrection was for him one instance of a general resurrection. He speaks of Jesus as 'the first fruits of those who have died'. Details of a body coming out of a tomb, or of a tomb being found empty or of visions, are all dramatic ways of expressing a faith in the power of God being available now to us through Jesus, unconfined by time or space.

Part D: Human Beings

18 Our Evolution

A FAMILIAR, TRADITIONAL UNDERSTANDING

- The human being is at the pinnacle of creation, for whom all else is created.

- We human beings were granted dominion over the Earth to use the natural world for our benefit.

A CONTEMPORARY UNDERSTANDING

- The human being is the most evolved species to appear on Earth, one among millions that share this planet.

- We human beings are not above the natural world but embedded within it. As evolved creatures with intelligence, we have a duty to care for it.

Our place as human beings in the Universe, and consequently upon Planet Earth, has undergone a great deal of rethinking over the last century or so. With the expansion of our scientific knowledge about the origin and the vastness of the Universe, we have shifted our thinking from our biblical tradition which was thought to provide us with ultimate truth about God, about Creation and about our place in it. From the literal reading of Genesis our beliefs ran like this. We were placed on a fixed, ready-made Earth over which we were to have dominion. As the only spiritual beings ('made in the image of God') we were intended to have a spiritual relationship with God and this was the only thing that ultimately mattered. All other beings in nature were purely material and put there for our use.

Today, our understanding of the time span of creation and of the vastness of the Universe puts us in a different relationship with everything around us.

Supposing we were to put the whole creation process, from the Big Bang (some 15 billion years ago), in the time scale of one year, we would have to say that human beings are very recent arrivals, within the last few seconds, so to speak. It is only in the sense that we are the latest arrivals, the most evolved creatures so far on Earth, that we can speak of ourselves as the 'crown' of creation. When we consider that 99% of all species that ever lived on this planet are now extinct it makes an absurdity of the idea that every species was created for our human use.

When we come to space, figures are literally astronomic. Our Earth is just one of nine planets that circle around one star (our Sun) which is one of some 10 billion stars in our galaxy – the Milky Way – which is one of some 10 billion galaxies. How tiny we are! When we look at a distant star at night we are looking back into history because what we see is not the star as it is today but as it was thousands of years ago when the light we see left it. This is all within the scope of what astro-physicists now know. We simply cannot know about, nor ever will, the regions of the Universe further than 15 billion light-years away because the light from such regions has not yet had time to reach Earth since the Big Bang!

Western science is now giving birth to a new creation story, a new cosmology. We humans are not separate beings *on* Earth but rather we are an expression *of* Earth. Pierre Teilhard de Chardin has written: 'The human person is the sum total of 15 billion years of unbroken evolution now thinking about itself'. This shift from seeing ourselves as separate beings placed on Earth to seeing ourselves as a conscious expression of Earth must cause a major shift in our understanding of who we are and of how we should respect and work *with* the whole of the natural world. We are caretakers, not masters.

This is the basis of the rising awareness today of ecological concerns, ranging from the depletion of the ozone layer to genetic engineering, and all matters 'green'. It also means that as Christians we have to adjust our orientation to understand that to be in accord with the will of God we have to align ourselves with the basic laws of evolution. Our being intelligent creatures puts on us the obligation of co-operating with God in the whole on-going creative process. What we are learning about our place in the Universe is the way in which God is revealing Himself and His purposes in our day. As Michael Dowd says in *Earthspirit*: 'We are seriously out of step with the Holy Spirit today, if we continue to read the Bible through the lens of the old cosmology. The most fundamental ways that we have of understanding ourselves, our world and how God relates to the whole process are shifting'.

Part D: Human Beings

19 The Fall

A FAMILIAR, TRADITIONAL UNDERSTANDING

- Humanity became enslaved to Satan by Adam and Eve's sin (the event known as 'The Fall') but has been set free by the blood of Christ.

A CONTEMPORARY UNDERSTANDING

- The world is part of an essentially good, evolving creation. Jesus' liberating act was not to right the past but to free us for our future evolution.

Until this century Christian doctrine has explained the Redemption as our being redeemed from a fallen state. But another way of understanding the early days of humanity is gaining ground as more in keeping with what we are discovering about human evolution. Instead of looking backwards to recover a glorious past, it understands the human journey as one which is ever moving forwards.

The Fall-Redemption spiritual tradition is now being replaced by a creation-centred one. While the former goes back to St Paul (eg. Romans 5), the creation-centred tradition traces its roots back centuries before the time of Jesus, to the earliest writers of the biblical books.

That the Fall-Redemption tradition considers all nature 'fallen' is due to the influence of the Gnostics in the early centuries of Church history. For them, all the world was evil, as a consequence of 'The Fall', and the only goodness was in the human soul, a spark of the Divine. So the world was regarded as hostile to us. This notion, particularly influenced by Manichaeism, reinforced the Greek dualistic notion that we are made up of body (evil) and soul (good). With such a paradigm, creation – and even our very bodies – are enemy number one.

Such a view is quite contrary to the biblical attitude to creation, which is very positive. Right from the Book of Genesis we read that as God took each step in the creating process He 'saw that it was good'. Psalm 104 is a hymn in praise of the Creator and of His creation. We notice that all the elements of creation are seen to be good in their own right, and not because they are good for or useful to humanity.

When the framework of our theology is Fall-Redemption then the benefits of the Jesus-event are understood to be directed backwards, to undoing a past evil. If our framework is creational then the Jesus-event is pointing towards, and enabling us on the way towards, what we have the potential to become. It is regarded as a step in human evolution. Jesus encouraged people to be instruments of a New Creation and even promised that we would do works (miracles) greater than his (John 14:12).

We have already seen in chapter 9 that the Adam and Eve myth is never referred to in the Hebrew Scriptures as a 'Fall'. When Scripture speaks of an angel with a sword at the gate of Paradise, it symbolically represents God's blessing upon our journey of evolving. There is no turning back: humanity had to move on.

There is no suggestion in Jesus' teaching that he himself believed in Original Sin, as we now understand it, since it was not a Jewish belief. Jesus himself, like the prophets before him, was forward-looking. To say, as some liturgical prayers do, that Jesus came to save us from our sins is to view him in a negative perspective: to appreciate him only in the context of sin. Whereas he came to establish our harmony with God, within ourselves, among us and between us and all creation. Not to restore but to raise up. As the great 13th century theologian Thomas Aquinas expressed it: 'The Son of God became human in order that humans might become gods and become the children of God'.

Another theological shift that is taking place within this new paradigm is to appreciate creation as an embodiment of the Divine.

The World has been described as 'the Body of God', that is, the outer manifestation of God. It acknowledges that God is not a power 'out there', but the *inner* dynamic guiding the creative process, the living reality living in and through creation. Except through the act of creating, God is not a creator. He 'needs' a creation to be a creator. This new understanding of God's relationship to creation has caused theologians to coin the word (from the Greek) *panentheism*. As different from the eastern belief of pantheism (that everything is God and God is everything), pan*en*theism means that God is *in* all creation and all creation is *in* God.

> 'Beloved, we are already the children of God but what we will be in the future has not yet been revealed. What we do know is this: when it is revealed we will be like him, for we will see him as he really is' (1 John 3:2).

Part D: Human Beings

20 Sin

A FAMILIAR, TRADITIONAL UNDERSTANDING

- Sin is an offence against God.

A CONTEMPORARY UNDERSTANDING

- Sin is a failure to grow in wholeness, within ourselves, with others and in relation to the whole of creation.

We cannot understand the notion of sin unless we first clarify what we mean by evil. First, we use the word loosely to describe anything which causes us to suffer. Disasters, whether natural (plagues, earthquakes) or human-caused (car crashes, Chernobyl-size explosions) are often referred to as physical evils. Then there is moral evil, the effects of deliberate human behaviour, which is our concern here. What seems an evil to one party may seem beneficial to another. For example the trade in slaves. Moral evil is a human creation, brought about by our pride, possessiveness, hatred, desire for revenge, envy, insecurity, lust for power: all arising from within us. There is no evil in the animal world because moral evil arises from free choice. When we see one animal in the wild tearing another to pieces in the most gruesome manner we think how cruel that is. It is not cruel. We project our human emotions on to the animal. It is simply acting out its nature. An animal can do no wrong! There is pain in the animal world, not cruelty. In the Universe's fifteen billion years of history, evil has only been around for the last half million or so.

Evil is a negativity arising from a misuse or excessive use of a positive energy. As a negative energy it has no existence in its own right. An analogy: we are only too familiar with holes of every shape and size, from the hole in our sock to a bomb crater. We would not deny their existence, yet in fact a hole has no existence of its own. It is an absence of something: a negativity. This does not mean we cannot experience evil's effect just as we can fall into a hole and break our neck.

It is a coincidence that *evil* is *live* spelt backwards in the English language! Evil is all that which is anti-life, anti-growth whether it be damaging to our personal growth towards fulfilment or preventing the growth of other people, or hampering the evolution of our planet, cosmic evil. While acknowledging that the presence of evil is not a necessary part of creation, we have to admit that in the process of human growth it is, however, inevitable. A child grows by expanding her experience outwards from a small world, rebelling against constraints, venturing beyond further boundaries. Rebellion is part of the process of growing up, in the course of which people inevitably get hurt. In humanity's own process of 'growing up' we cause wastage, breakage, damage and destruction.

Christians refer to evil acts as sins. But we have to ask, are some forms of behaviour labelled sinful because God has decreed that they are? Or has society found that certain behaviour is injurious to human well-being and therefore invoked the authority of God to enforce a taboo? Did God launch humanity onto this Earth with a fixed set of rules or did God wish us to work out our manner of living in harmony with ourselves and with nature as we went along? The fact that different cultures live by different sets of 'commandments' would point to the latter.

If we were taught at an early age that 'sin is an offence against God' this coloured the development of our personal scale of values. There was the implication, which in our innocence we automatically took on board, that everything our parents taught us to be wrong or bad was sinful and therefore displeasing to God – even such misdemeanours as not saying 'please' or forgetting to wash our hands. We were reprimanded for these, so they must be morally wrong and therefore sinful and therefore hurting God. Or so we may have reasoned. This notion of sin gave birth to a concept of a God who is to be feared because eventually it will be not our parents but God who will punish us.

Despite what might have been taught in Sunday School or Catechism class, we cannot hurt or displease or anger God. If we were able to influence God's attitude towards us – and this is as true of pleasing God as of displeasing God – we would have a power over God.

So how are we to understand sin? We can only speak of something being an offence against God analogously if it is an offence against humanity or against our own potential, our future growth: against God's design for creation. In other words, sin is a breakdown in relationships, with others or with our environment. The word *sin* is shorthand for the destruction or rejection of love. We cannot sin against God directly. We can only sin and bring about the consequences of sin within the context within which we live.

Unlike our ancestors, we today are more aware of our relationship to other people than to God and consequently we are more likely to think of sin in terms of what effect our actions have on our relationship with our neighbours than on our relationship with God.

Only the person offended can grant forgiveness. There can be no meaning in asking forgiveness of God for our sin unless we also ask forgiveness of those whom our sin has offended. To ask our offended neighbour for forgiveness is much more difficult, more soul-purifying, than simply to mumble an Act of Contrition to God. This is the beginning of reconciliation. Very often the first step towards reconciliation has to be a forgiveness of ourselves, for in the first place it is we ourselves who have been damaged by our own evil acts.

Part D: Human Beings

21 Judgement

A FAMILIAR, TRADITIONAL UNDERSTANDING	A CONTEMPORARY UNDERSTANDING
• We obey the Commandments in order to receive our reward in the next life.	• We try to be loving people because we believe this leads to our own and all Creation's fulfilment.

The only way we can relate to the ineffable, the mystery we call 'God', is by projecting onto the Divine Being the human virtues we value such as beauty, justice, freedom, truth. But we go even further and imagine God acting as we human beings act, being angry, judgmental and punishing. Christians have inherited some of these concepts from the Hebrew Scriptures. For instance, we think of God as a jealous God ('I am the Lord your God and I tolerate no rivals' Exodus 20:5) as punishing us for offending Him ('I will not fail to punish children and grand-children to the third and fourth generation for the sins of their parents' Exodus 34:7). This is the way human beings would act so it was presumed God would act in the same way. Similarly, there will be a day of reckoning: 'He calls heaven and earth as witnesses to see him judge his people' (Psalm 50 [49]).

But more than this, we imagine God punishing us in the way we punish each other, so often vindictively: 'The punishment shall be life for life, eye for eye, tooth for tooth, hand for hand, foot for foot, burn for burn, wound for wound, bruise for bruise' (Exodus 21:23-25). This is what Moses understood God wanted to teach His people. However, the intention was not to tell them how vindictive they could be but to say this is the maximum punishment they might extract. Despite what Jesus said about forgiveness 'Do not take revenge on someone who wrongs you' (Matthew 5:38-39) and we should forgive 'not seven times but seventy times seven' (Matthew 18:22) we still act vindictively. Our prisons are regarded by the general public, not primarily as places for improvement but as places for punishment. How often have we heard the victim of an assault, interviewed on television, say: 'He caused suffering so he must be made to suffer'.

God does not need to be vindictive! God does not punish us. We are punished *by* our sins, not *for* our sins. We are 'punished' by suffering the consequences of our wrong-doing. Such suffering is of value to us only if we recognise it and accept it as a lesson for our future.

We are fearful of anger and judgement and punishment so we are fearful of God. So many of us have received our Christian formation on the basis of 'The fear of the Lord is the beginning of wisdom' (Psalm 111:10). The phrase 'fear of the Lord' which occurs so frequently in the Jewish Testament is hardly ever mentioned in the New Testament and only once on the lips of Jesus (Luke 12:5). The word 'fear' is better translated by 'awe' or 'respect' or 'admiration'. (The Good News Bible translates that verse of the psalm as: 'The way to become wise is to honour the Lord'.)

The idea of a Last Judgement is a subject which the classical artists have really exploited. Their paintings feed our imaginations with images of celestial weighing-scales upon which are loaded all the good deeds of our life and all the evil deeds. Then there is a fearful hush in the heavenly court while we and the angelic choirs hold our breath as we wait to see which way the scales tip, and then … a judgement is pronounced which will determine our eternity! No wonder many people are so afraid of death.

The evil we have created – but also the good and love we have created – are not cumulative in the sense of our putting them into a celestial deposit account. They affect us here and now. They make us what we are today. Their only influence on us as we face death lies in how they have caused us to become the loving or hating people we are at the moment of dying.

It is an acknowledged piece of folklore that when you are drowning your past life flashes before your eyes. Many researchers into the 'near-death experience' believe that the life review is a common feature of that experience. Maybe the idea of a judgement at death owes its origin to this. Dr. Peter Fenwick in his book *The Truth in the Light* in which he reports on an investigation of over 300 near-death experiences, speaks of the classical life review

> 'in which a person is shown his or her life in a panoramic fashion. Although actions which have been carried out are often seen as shabby and self-interested, the person does not feel judged; guilt is made more tolerable by the supportive quality of the surrounding light of love.'

And this is how Jesus explains it:

> 'Whoever believes in the Son is not judged; but whoever does not believe has already been judged because he has not believed in God's Son. This is how the judgement works: the light has come into the world, but people love the darkness rather than the light, because their deeds are evil. Anyone who does evil things hates the light and will not come to the light, because he does not want his evil deeds to be shown up. But whoever does what is true comes to the light in order that the light may show that what he did was in obedience to God' (John 3:18-21).

We are 'obedient to God' when our wills are in harmony with the way in which the Divine Will is manifested to us through the continuing day-by-day process of creation. Living thus brings us and Creation to fulfilment.

Part D: Human Beings

22 The Way

A FAMILIAR, TRADITIONAL UNDERSTANDING	A CONTEMPORARY UNDERSTANDING
• Belief in Jesus as one's personal Saviour is the essence of being a Christian.	• Following the way of love shown by Jesus is the essence of being a Christian.

It is only in the languages of the western world that we find a word for 'religion'. Yet other cultures are not less religious. On the contrary, they have no word for it because they are more religious in the sense that they do not make the distinction between the sacred and the profane. Religion is part of all aspects of their life. They do not regard life with the dualism that we do in the West. We distinguish the spiritual from the material, the holy from the profane, the sacred from the secular. And from this follows the distinction between body and soul so that children are taught from an early age that they possess a body and a soul and that the latter is more important than the former because the latter is eternal.

Since the Enlightenment in Europe in the 18th century stressing the supremacy of reason over faith, religion became a very private affair. A person's relationship with God, or even their beliefs, were not subjects of conversation. Religion became something private, just between me and God. The social dimension of religion was lost. So it is not surprising that the spiritual and religious element of living became separated from the rest of life.

Two things had been forgotten. First, that apart from words, there is no way we can express our love of God, other than through the way we express our love of other people. Our words, however piously said in prayer, are empty unless given substance in the way we behave. Secondly, Jesus was more concerned about the way people lived and related than in what they believed. The essence of his Kingdom message was not about new beliefs but about a new way of relating: of demonstrating our love of God by our love of our neighbour (Matthew 22:37-40).

In the first centuries of Christianity the message of Jesus was influenced by the Gnostic teaching that all in the world was evil, as a consequence of 'The Fall', and that the only goodness was in the human soul: a spark of the Divine. So the world was hostile to us. Such a view is quite contrary to the biblical attitude towards creation, which is very positive. In our secular society today our world is regarded as neither good nor bad but neutral. The Earth is there for our use, to be pillaged, raped: it is just raw material for economic growth, technological development, scientific discovery. Nature, though not evil, is there to be conquered and dominated so that we human beings may evolve independently towards our own perfection. Surprisingly, this attitude is not the child of 18th century rationalism but could be said to have originated from Thomas Aquinas in the 13th century. Anxious to move from the earlier Gnostic negative view of the world and of the human body, he taught that the world is not just neutral but good. However, it is good, not on its own account, but only because it serves our human needs. The body is good only in so far as it is at the service of the soul.

When religion came to be regarded as essentially 'otherness', taken out of the context of everyday life, the concentration of religious practice was upon 'saving my soul'. Life on Earth was no longer valued for itself but as simply a preparation for Heaven. In the ever-popular *Spiritual Exercises of St Ignatius* written in the 16th century we read:

> 'Man has been created to praise, reverence and serve our Lord God, thereby saving his soul. Everything else on Earth has been created for man's sake, to enable him to achieve the purpose for which he was created.'

There is a growing reaction to this stance today in the expression of environmental and ecological concerns and it is being forced upon us by our awakening to the disastrous effects of the way we treat our Planet and what this might lead to. Within the Christian tradition, in our materialist West, there is a growing awareness of the sacredness of creation. Thanks to the resurgence of Celtic Spirituality and the inspiration of Creation Theology we are coming to an appreciation of all creation, in its micro and macro dimensions, being a reflection of the Creator and having a value for itself, of which humanity is a part.

Perhaps it is this new appreciation of our oneness with all creation that will cause Christianity to give importance to 'whole-life' rather than simply to 'soul-life': that it is not belief and worship that is of primary importance but our loving service in the world for the well-being of others and for the whole of creation.

Part D: Human Beings

23 Grace

A FAMILIAR, TRADITIONAL UNDERSTANDING

- The grace of the Holy Spirit has the power to justify us, cleanse us of our sins. It is a gratuitous gift we receive through Baptism.

A CONTEMPORARY UNDERSTANDING

- Grace is our participation in God's creative energy. It is God's gift to every human being.

Ask any non-church person what the word "grace" means and they will reply "poise", "elegance", "charm" or "favour" as in "grace and favour accommodation".

For the Christian, the word "grace" has a God-dimension. We learnt as children that there are two kinds of supernatural grace. Sanctifying Grace which is an habitual disposition to participate in the Divine life and Actual Grace which is God's intervention assisting us in our work of sanctification. This is very theoretical and not very inspiring! To give this theological concept a relevance in our everyday life, we can think of grace in terms of energy.

Energy is manifested in many different forms, of which wave-motion or radiation, is one. We observe it from the low frequency physical energy in steam that used to drive our locomotives, through radio, TV and microwaves, through the spectrum of visible colours, to cosmic rays and healing energies to the highest frequency of creative energy which we call Love. Operating at different frequencies the radiation of energy causes different effects.

All matter is a manifestation of energy. Consequently, energy is the great unifier. It is through energy that everything in creation is inter-related and inter-dependent.

Creation is the continuous bursting forth of Divine Energy. The Big Bang was an explosion of energy: an explosion of Love given material form.

Physicists speak of all energy existing in two forms. It is either Potential (stored) Energy or Kinetic (moving) Energy. Water in a dam provides an apt illustration of this distinction. The water contains Potential Energy by virtue of its being constrained by the dam. If water is released from the dam this Potential Energy is converted into Kinetic Energy.

We can compare Potential Energy with our "participation in the life of God", with Sanctifying Grace, being in a state of energy. While Kinetic Energy can be compared with the activation of this gift in our lives, Actual Grace, in the myriad ways in which we expend energy. Seen this way, we overcome the dualism of what is natural and what is supernatural. All is energy. All is of God.

We can apply to ourselves the gift of Justification by understanding it not as forgiveness, but rather as the gift of a healing energy, an empowerment, so that "we shall become mature people, reaching to the very height of the Christ's full stature" (Eph. 4:13). The healing, growth-giving energy is already ours as Potential Energy. It requires to be drawn upon. Just as the work of natural healers – whether using Reflexology, Acupuncture, Reiki or any other method – is not to add anything to a person but to balance the life-giving energies we already possess so that they operate in harmony and so restore our bodily deficiencies. God's creative energy is a healing energy.

"I have come so that they may have life – life in all its fullness" (John 10:10). The Greek text uses the word *zoee* here (for *life*) which carries a sense of aliveness or physical energy, so: "I have come so that they may have energy", the Divine Energy, Eternal Life.

Consciousness is one manifestation of energy. Every action (thought) of the brain generates a minuscule amount of energy. Synergy (sy-energy) – many minds acting in coherence – can produce a morphic field effect as has been demonstrated by the benefits it brings to the surroundings by people meditating together in large groups.

God, in His continuing creative action is the source of all energy. So we can say, with Church teaching, that creative energy/grace is God's free and undeserved gift to us. There is no other source of energy than Divine Energy. Since we owe our existence to this source it is a participation in the life of God.

If we say God is the source of energy, can we say "God is energy"? If we think of God Manifest (to use a Hindu term) as the Universe with all its workings and of God Unmanifest as the intelligence, the consciousness, that is driving the workings of the manifest Universe, then God Unmanifest corresponds to Potential Energy (the water in the dam) and God Manifest to Kinetic Energy (the water released). Everything that goes on in the Universe is God made manifest by the conversion of God's unmanifest Potential Energy into manifest Kinetic Energy.

Just as we cannot see energy, so we cannot see God. We see, we experience, the effects of energy. We experience the effects of God. If such a way of conceiving that which is inconceivable, namely God, feels too impersonal, let us remember that we human beings reflect, as only human beings can, God's highest attributes: supreme consciousness and unconditional love, both of which are manifestations of energy.

We are minute reflections of these attributes. We are sinners, yes. But we are not sinful, we are graceful: we are God-full!

Part E: The Church

24 The Kingdom of God

A FAMILIAR, TRADITIONAL UNDERSTANDING	A CONTEMPORARY UNDERSTANDING
• The Church is an organisation, superior to civil society because matters spiritual are superior to matters temporal.	• The Church is called to be an expression on Earth – a sign or witness – of what it means to live by the values of what Jesus called the Kingdom of God.

At different times in its two thousand year's history the Church has presented different faces and been through a variety of relationships with civil society.

With the destruction of Jerusalem and the Second Temple in 70 CE by the Romans, the followers of 'The Way', as they came to be called, fled from their own country and made a cultural leap out of Judaism. The enormity of this leap, taken by the small new Jewish sect, out of Palestine onto the stage of the then known world, is easily overlooked. For one thing, it would seem that Jesus himself had not foreseen that his proposed new way of living and relating should reach beyond the Jewish nation. He exhorted his contemporaries to become better Jews, to fulfil the law of Moses (Matthew 5:17). 'It is from the Jews that salvation comes' he said (John 4:22). He was culturally conditioned to believe that God's blessings came only through the Jewish race. Were they not, after all, God's Chosen People? (It is true, there are other verses in the gospel – eg. Matthew 10:18, 24:14, 28:19 – which would seem to indicate that Jesus was expecting his disciples to preach to the Gentile world too. But we must remember that the Gospels were written years after *The Way* had spread into Asia Minor so it is quite likely that these words were not actually uttered by Jesus.) As his followers moved out of Palestine into Asia Minor they at first preached to their fellow Jews, then later as the number of Gentile members grew they broke altogether with the synagogue and called themselves the *ekklesia,* the assembly, 'the Church'.

As the community grew in numbers and in geographical extent it became institutionalised and began to show the characteristics of a new religion, alongside the Jewish religion and the religion of pagan Rome. As it spread through the Roman Empire it engendered suspicion and became the subject of persecution. In 321 Constantine became the first Christian Emperor (although some historians believe his motivation was purely political) and from then on Christianity really took off all over the Roman Empire. The early Christian theologian Origen (c185-c254) sadly acknowledged that as Christianity became an established religion, so it became corrupt. (In the middle of the 3rd century a wealthy woman called Lucilla actually paid to have her servant Majorinus made Bishop of Carthage!) The Church required organisation so it copied that of the Roman Empire.

It has been said that Jesus gave us the Kingdom of God but what we got was the Church! The simplicity of the announcement of the Good News in Palestine encountered the Greek world of the philosophers where it became intellectualised. The Lutheran theologian Adolf von Harnack summed up this development: 'When the Messiah became Logos the Gospel became theology'. Having lost sight of its purpose vis-a-vis the Kingdom of God, the heart of Jesus' message, the Church exercised its presence in the world in ways which we can now judge as being detrimental to rather than supportive of the values of the Kingdom. Not only did Kingdom and Church become identified but Kingdom and Empire: the Empire of Christendom. It is said that Charlemagne saw himself as the new David and had his throne in Aachen modelled after the throne of Solomon. As the Church gained secular influence, there was the presumption that Popes and Bishops should possess a power parallel to, and in some cases greater than, the temporal rulers in order to fulfil their spiritual office. Pope Innocent II in the 13th century was the most powerful ruler in the whole of Europe. In 1302 Pope Boniface VIII declared himself to be the most powerful man in the world with the right to rule over kings! In the Bull *Unam Sanctam* he declared that 'every human creature must be subject to the Roman Pontiff'. Between the 12th and 17th centuries most European bishops ruled over large estates and even over whole regions of a country. Of the eight 'electors' of the Emperor in Germany, four were bishops who had this right because they were rulers of provinces.

A second form of misuse of power, this time spiritual, was that employed to preserve the supremacy of the Christian faith: the Crusades in order to destroy the 'Infidel' and the Inquisition as a treatment for heretics. (Both were exercised because of concern for the individual's salvation!) From the 15th century onwards, the Church identified with the morality of the trading or middle classes, a characteristic that can still be noticed, whether it be in the support of the 'rights' of landowners or its dubious speculations on the world financial market.

Despite this counter-witness of the Kingdom values, there is a great movement through all the Churches today to re-think the nature of the Church, its mission and its place in secular society. The various new models of the Church being suggested today use expressions like 'a pilgrim people' a 'servant Church', a 'sign of the Kingdom'. The Sri Lanken theologian Tissa Balasuriya reminds us (in *Planetary Theology*): 'The principal mission of Christians and the Churches as communities of believers is to foster the conditions for the self-realisation and fulfilment of each and every person and for the full flowering of nature.' And Dom Bede Griffiths, the Benedictine monk who settled in an ashram in India, wrote in *Return to the Centre*: 'The organisation of the Church ... has no other purpose than to communicate love, to create a community of love, to unite all people in the eternal Ground of being, which is present in the heart of everyone. This is the criterion by which the

Church is to be judged, not by the forms of its doctrine or ritual, but by the reality of the love which it manifests.'

Part E: The Church

25 Hierarchy or Community

A FAMILIAR, TRADITIONAL UNDERSTANDING

- The Church is hierarchical in structure. Members relate according to their authority roles.

A CONTEMPORARY UNDERSTANDING

- The Church is a community. The fundamental relationship of all Christians is as sisters and brothers in a common humanity.

The essence of living the Kingdom values, which it is the Church's role to reflect and promote, lies in acknowledging that God is the common Father of all humanity and that subsequently we have to relate to all people as our sisters and brothers. However, this is not the way it is – even in the Church.

Whenever we human beings live together we need to form a social structure. The early Church took on the structure of society of the time which was a patriarchal and hierarchical society, a social structure that goes back more than 4,000 years and is with us still. Our present world economy is based upon the few dominating the many. It is a power structure.

It seems to have become the pattern for society when our ancestors took the evolutionary step from being hunter-gatherers and developed skills in agriculture and animal husbandry. This demanded more stable communities needing to possess land they could call their own and defend against invaders. This meant the need to fight, the requirement of male warriors. So male supremacy developed.

Jesus' ancestors, the Semitic people who invaded Canaan from the South, were nomadic herdsmen ruled by warriors and priests, the Levites, who brought with them a male god of war: Jehovah or Yahweh. Given this social structure in Israel it is understandable why the Christ had to appear among us as Jesus the male rather than in a female role.

But Jesus proposed a different model. His idea for humanity was so radical, he was able to envisage how it could be otherwise. Sadly though, only a few years after Pentecost, Jesus' small group of followers were so unable to situate themselves in another social shape than that around them that they began to organise their converts on the pattern of the contemporary civil state and themselves to assume the role in the new community that the Saducees and Pharisees were playing in the Jewish nation. And it has been evident in the Church ever since. The very word 'hierarchy' was coined by Dionysius, a 6th century monk in Syria, to denote the totality of ruling persons in the Church. Hierarchy means 'sacred government' and we speak of those with power in ecclesiastical society, the bishops, as 'The Hierarchy', from whom instructions, doctrines and precepts filter down.

Jesus' Kingdom vision cut right through the traditions of his culture and he challenged people – and us – to see that there is another way of ordering our relationships. Nowhere in the gospels do we find Jesus approving the hierarchy model. To the future leaders of his community he said:

> 'You know that the men who are considered to be rulers
> of the heathen have power over them, and the leaders
> have complete authority. This, however, is not the way it is
> among you. If one of you wants to be great he must be the
> servant of the rest' (Mark 10:42-45).

Hierarchical society values us for what we *have* or what we can contribute from what we have: our role, our abilities, our leadership, our honours and titles, our education, our class or caste. We are what we are only by being measured against others. Even our self-worth depends upon how others regard us. By contrast, the

Kingdom pattern of society values us for what we *are*. Our worth comes from our being of value to and beloved by God because there is that of God in us. Jesus valued children as highly as adults (Mark 10:13-16). He had no time for the pomp of the 'teachers of the law and the Pharisees' (Matthew 23:6-10). He did not treat women as being in any way inferior to men. He had special concern for the marginalised, the outcasts, for lepers, for the public sinners, for the despised tax-collectors. Roles played no part in the way he valued people.

And now, two thousand years on, we begin to see encouraging signs that humanity is taking small steps to move from a hierarchical society towards a community society. The model is changing from that of a pyramid to be more like that of a honeycomb. For a whole variety of reasons the authority of 'authority figures' is being questioned. Just because a person is a teacher or a parent or a minister of religion or a politician it does not follow that we owe them blind obedience. A more highly educated population wants to make its own responsible decisions. Democracy, practised as a means of subsidiarity and consensus government, is sought world-wide. Those 'in authority' have to be accountable. And today we witness a reaction against male domination and a desire for every person, no matter what their sex, race, colour, religion, to have equal opportunities. Respect for the individual's worth, their 'human rights', is a preliminary step towards forming a communitarian society – Jesus' Kingdom society – in which everyone's intrinsic worth is valued.

Part E: The Church

26 God's Spirit

A FAMILIAR, TRADITIONAL UNDERSTANDING

- The Holy Spirit distributes God's grace through the Church.

A CONTEMPORARY UNDERSTANDING

- The Spirit of God inspires all people of good will in different ways and through different events throughout history.

In 1968 the World Council of Churches published a document entitled "The Church for Others". In one place it says:

'In the past it has been customary to maintain that God is related to the world through the Church. When we sharpen this view into a formula the sequence would be: God – Church – World. This has been understood to mean that God is primarily related to the Church and only secondarily to the world by means of the Church. Further, it has been held that God relates himself to the world through the Church in order to gather everyone possible from the world into the Church. God, in other words, moves through the Church to the world. We believe that the time has come to question this sequence and to emphasise an alternative. According to this alternative the last two items in God – Church – World should be reversed, so that it reads instead God – World – Church. That is, God's primary relationship is to the world, and it is the world and not the Church that is the focus of God's plan.'

It is understandable how the first formula came to be accepted in the first millennium of the Church when much of the known world was thought of as Christendom and there was almost no other option than to be a Christian. In today's pluralistic society with our sense of the world as a global village in which we are daily encountering people of other religions, or none, we can no longer accept that the Church – and in this case we mean Church Ministers, the Hierarchy – should control the workings of the Holy Spirit: control the 'tap' which supplies God's grace!

We see so many signs of goodness, of love of neighbour, around us in the lives of adherents of other Faiths and among people, for instance of the African Traditional religions who have never heard of Christ or the Church. These are signs that the Spirit is free to 'blow where She wills' and can be neither contained nor controlled by any human agency. The Spirit was clearly active in Jewish history (our Old Testament times) long before the Church came into being.

One of the documents issuing from the Second Vatican Council of the World's Catholic Bishops in the sixties, states:

> 'The People of God (ie. the Church) motivated by faith,
> labours to decipher authentic signs of God's presence and
> purpose in the happenings, needs and desires in which this
> People has a part along with other men of our age.'

This task of all Christians is to 'read the signs of the times', which in its biblical sense means looking for signs of the Spirit's action in the world working, through human agency, towards God's final intention for His creation – what Jesus referred to as the Reign of God.

This is not the same as saying that the Church should follow every fashion and fad of the modern world in order to be attractive or more acceptable. But it does mean that the whole Church – all Christians – are called to exercise their prophetic role in the world. This has nothing to do with foretelling the future. It means that we have always to identify the major trends in society evident 'in the happenings, needs and desires' and put them under the scrutiny of the Word of God. In other words, to make a judgement about these trends in the light of Scripture and then discern which we consider to be furthering the Reign of God and which are militating against it. In a nutshell: which are making people more fully human, more loving, enabling them to become the human persons God created them to become, and which trends oppose this.

But the call of the Christian does not stop with this discernment. To exercise our prophetic role we have then to be agents of the Holy Spirit by supporting, putting our weight behind those trends in contemporary society which favour the Reign of God and equally by condemning, opposing those which are clearly not of the Spirit.

The role of the Church is not to control the Spirit's actions but to be the leaven in the dough, enabling the action of the Spirit to be fruitful in the world.

Part E: The Church

27 Theology, Science and Religion

A FAMILIAR, TRADITIONAL UNDERSTANDING

- Theology is the prerogative of the teaching authority of the Church.

- Religion and science cannot both be true.

A CONTEMPORARY UNDERSTANDING

- Theology is everyone's concern. It is the formulation of our deepest spiritual experience, our exploration into God.

- Religion and science provide different perspectives for comprehending Truth. They cannot be in contradiction.

Theology is the way we think about God and matters Divine. It is the work of the rational mind dealing with religious experience. It is head stuff. It is what we are doing in these pages. St Anselm described it as 'Faith seeking understanding'. It is not the prerogative of the professionals we call Theologians.

As soon as our early ancestors became self-reflective, had arrived at a sense of their own identity, they began to rationalise and to differentiate past from present from future – this was with the development of a rudimentary language – and fundamental questions began to be asked. Who are we? Why are we here? What is our origin? What is our value? What is there beyond death? These are theological questions. Myths arose to supply answers. Myth is the seed of theology. The origin myth is the most fundamental story of all societies. It has been defined as a sacred narrative explaining how the world and human beings came to be in their present form and condition. The mythologist Joseph Campbell wrote:

> 'We find that such themes as the fire-thief, the flood, a
> land of the dead, a virgin birth and a resurrection hero
> have a world-wide distribution – appearing everywhere in
> new combinations, while remaining, like the elements of a
> kaleidoscope, only a few and always the same.'

In his book *The Chosen Peoples* missiologist Walbert Bühlmann makes the point that tribes and societies the world over have considered themselves to be 'chosen', to be favoured in a special way by their supreme deity who defends them against their neighbouring tribes. And so, as we know, did the Israelites. Yet through the mouth of the prophet Amos God reminds them:

> 'People of Israel are not you and the Cushites [Ethiopians]
> all the same to me? Did not I, who brought Israel out of the
> land of Egypt, bring the Philistines from Caphtor and the
> Aramaeans from Kir?' (Amos 9:7.)

The expression of a people's religious experience is always in terms of their history and their culture. So one cannot take literally and interpret with today's vocabulary the expression of a spiritual experience formulated in another age and another culture. Theology, then, is a living study, with its formulations needing constant revision. We cannot even speak of *the* Christian theology. There are always many theologies abroad: Scholastic, Reformation, Contextual, Liberation, Creation, Feminist, etc, each issuing from a particular point of view.

Today there is often thought to be a contradiction – opposition even – between theology (religion) and science. In the Middle Ages the influence of the Church was such that it was the current biblical interpretation of the material world which shaped 'scientific' thinking. The monks were the scholars of the Middle Ages and there was no question of their allowing rival theories abroad. We know what happened to free-thinking men like Copernicus and Galileo! Science, as an accepted discipline, has appeared only very recently in our history. It really only came into its own in the 17th century.

Both the scientist and the theologian search for Truth; search for a rationally motivated belief about the way things are. Their respective paths are not in opposition: they run in parallel. Scientific and biblical statements can both be true, but they are expressing truth in different terms. For instance, I could describe an ice-cream quite objectively in terms of its chemical components or I could describe it subjectively in terms of how I perceive its colour, its taste, its meaning to me as a food.

Since the turn of the century scientists have been discovering such amazing things about the Universe, in both micro and macro directions, that they have contributed to our thinking about the mystery we call God. Paul, writing to the Christians in Rome, said:

> 'Ever since God created the world, his invisible qualities, both his eternal power and his divine nature, have been clearly seen; they are perceived in the things that God has made' (1:20).

From this can be inferred that the evolutionary process is from the beginning a spiritual as well as a physical process. While many scientists today are awakening to the numinous quality of the Universe and approaching it with a sense of wonder, theologians are (as we saw in Chapters 8 and 19) moving from concern for a flawed world to emphasising the positive aspects of creation. This is the moment when scientists and mystics draw closer together. It was Einstein who said: 'Religion without science is blind. Science without religion is lame'.

Part E: The Church

28 Spiritual Authority

A FAMILIAR, TRADITIONAL UNDERSTANDING

- The Church is the ultimate arbiter of Divine Truth.

A CONTEMPORARY UNDERSTANDING

- The Spirit speaks to us with many different voices.

One of the problems of a religion as sophisticated and as morally powerful as Christianity is that it conditions us at an early age into a particular way of thinking. Those concepts that we imbibed in our early years sank deep roots and to attempt to change our mind-set in later life calls for a fundamental, and often courageous re-orientation. It is a re-orientation of our outlook, of the meaning we give to life, much more than exchanging old ideas for new, or updating our present thinking.

This mental shift is illustrated when the question is posed to people: 'Are you afraid of God?'. After a pause they will, sometimes hesitantly, say 'No'. This is a head answer. Not an answer from the gut-level. For many, on account of their early religious upbringing, when fear of divine punishment was used as a method of control, it takes months, sometimes years, struggling with this question before they can say 'No' with complete integrity and peace of heart.

One of the major differences between Western and Eastern religious thinking is that in the Eastern religions great value is given to inner spiritual experience, while in the West the emphasis has been on external authority in religious matters. It has not always been so. As an undercurrent to more orthodox thinking there has been an appreciation of the mystical in the West from earliest times. We find it in the Gnostic traditions within Christianity which were ruthlessly repressed in the 13th century. There are more recent echoes of it in the ideas of such Western philosophers as Berkeley, Bergson, William James and A.N.Whitehead. Aldous Huxley spoke of it as forming part of what he termed the 'perennial wisdom', the esoteric strand of thought and practice that underlies and unites the mystical elements in all the great spiritual traditions.

Among several reasons why this alternative approach to spirituality failed to influence Western thinking is our insistence that intellectual orthodoxy and obedience to temporal authority are necessary partners. This outlook had its nurturing in the adoption by the Emperor Constantine in the 4th century of Christianity as the official religion of the Roman Empire. During succeeding centuries the Church, in its role as guardian of literacy and learning, came to provide the temporal rulers with increasingly necessary clerical and administrative support. In this way, the Church gained widespread control over what could and could not be thought and expressed. This increased both its own and the State's power of social and political control. In consequence, the Church felt threatened by any movements which claimed that women and men could find God for themselves without the guidance or ministry of a hierarchical priesthood. Gnostics were condemned as heretics, excommunications were frequent and the Church reacted with the authorised brutality of the Inquisition.

Mystics have always been regarded with suspicion and marginalised during their lifetime. Their experience of God is such that it is at a different level of consciousness from knowledge about God. It is a direct encounter with Ultimate Reality such that it is self-authenticating and is not dependent upon external authority to confirm its truth.

In the East, things were different. The great spiritual traditions of Hinduism, Buddhism, Jainism, Taoism never became servants of secular regimes and remained essentially inward-looking and self-reflective. Even in Tibet, where spiritual and temporal authority were combined in the same individuals and institutions, there was little mind control. Buddhism emphasised salvation by enlightenment through the activities of one's own mind, not through the actions or instructions of its priests.

So there has developed in our world two distinct ways of engaging with the spiritual: primarily outwards as in the West, primarily inwards as in the East. But in our present day they need not be thought to be in opposition. They can be experienced as complementing one another. We in the West are coming into increasing contact with the cultures and customs of the East, and beginning to appreciate how their spiritual wisdom can enhance our own lives.

Increasingly, for instance, Westoners are being attracted to the different methods of meditation that have their origin and tradition in Asia. In recent years Christian monks from Europe have come to understand how their spirituality is enriched by deepening their understanding of the Hindu approach to the Eastern spirituality and meditative traditions.

We in the West have so much to gain if we are able to admit that ours is not the only way to approach the Divine, but are prepared to investigate another way. We no longer have to travel to the East for this. The East has come to us. It is up to us to be adventurous and enter into dialogue with our new neighbours. But do we have the courage to respect our intuition, to be open to wherever this may lead? We should take advice from the Letter to the Hebrews: 'Let us go forward to mature teaching and leave behind us the first lessons [we learnt] of the Christian message' (6:1)

Part E: The Church

29 Unity and Diversity

A FAMILIAR, TRADITIONAL UNDERSTANDING

- Because we believe our Church has the true interpretation of Divine Revelation, 'we should act separately in all matters except where we are compelled to act together'

A CONTEMPORARY UNDERSTANDING

- We 'should act together in all matters except those in which deep differences of conviction compel us to act separately'. (World Council of Churches, Lund Assembly. 1952)

Today there are reckoned to be 423 different Christian denominations in the world. This may sadden us but it should not surprise us. We have already said (chapter 26) that there is not one Christian theology. In the course of Christian history various social and cultural shifts have presented different images of Christ. In the first centuries, when the bishops were establishing themselves, Christ was depicted as the Good Shepherd guiding the flock to its heavenly home. After Constantine's conversion the Christ was pictured as the victor over death, the ruler of the world. During the medieval period when the Church was the vehicle of both social and cultural change it was Christ's ascent from the cross to be the judge of humanity which was to the fore. Then came the Gothic Christ, the Christ of the crucifix and in our own time the Cosmic Christ and the feminine Christ. In the same way, there are also many theologies proposed by different Churches depending upon their differing interpretations of Scripture.

Going back to sources, this should not surprise us either because, as we saw in chapter 13, there never was one orthodox doctrine of

Jesus: Paul, Matthew, Mark, Luke and John all present different portraits. Some modern authors have tried to put these witnesses together and form just one chronological gospel story. It does not work. They were never meant as diaries. Their accounts are full of contradictions. Even our official statement of Christian faith, the Nicene Creed, does not give us a full picture: it jumps straight from the birth of Jesus to his death, omitting that most crucial part of his life: his announcement of the bursting forth of the Kingdom of God.

We might believe that the first split in the Christian family occurred in the 11th century when the Eastern Orthodox Churches split off from the western Roman Church. The split we are more familiar with in the West is that of the Reformation in 16th century Europe which began with an attempt to reform the Roman Church and resulted in the establishment of the Protestant Churches.

However, right from the earliest days, Christians were divided among themselves. The first followers of Jesus, under James and Peter, founded the Jerusalem Church after Jesus' death. In all their beliefs they were indistinguishable from the Pharisees, except that they believed in the resurrection of Jesus and that Jesus was the promised Messiah. They believed he would soon come back to complete his mission of overthrowing the Romans and setting up the Messianic Kingdom. The first leader of this Jerusalem Church was James, the brother of Jesus. They did not regard themselves as belonging to any new religion: their religion was Judaism.

Paul, who had never known Jesus in his earthly life, developed another line, away from normal Judaism and that of the Jerusalem Church. He can be said to have been the cause of Christianity developing as a new religion, based on the idea of an atoning death of a Divine Being. He made the crucifixion of Jesus the centre of his thinking. It was Paul who first deified Jesus: the historical Jesus became Christ the redeemer. Rather than having a Jewish perspective, he framed his message about the Christ in terms borrowed from the Hellenist mystic cults. The rifts between the Jerusalem Church and the Asia Minor Church were much greater than would appear from the Acts of the Apostles. (The first hint is given in Acts 15.) While the apostles – as different from 'the Twelve' of the gospels – stayed in Jerusalem, Paul's group became missionary, which is why the Christian theology we know developed from Paul's preaching, just as the gospels were influenced by the theology of his letters. How often in the epistles we find Paul saying: 'my gospel' or 'the gospel announced by me'. The Church grew from these roots. We hear little more about the Jerusalem Church.

Today we are more conscious of the scandal our divisions present to a secular world, and so there is a great movement of ecumenism abroad, based on the notion that what unites us is more important than what divides us. What divisions exist between Christians are much less on a vertical plane – between Presbyterians, Baptists, Anglicans, Catholics, Methodists, etc – than on a horizontal plane cutting across denominations: between ecumenists and fundamentalists, charismatics and meditators, radicals and conservatives. Our differences no longer focus so much on statements of belief as on the way in which we experience our Christian life. The Churches are not seeking a uniformity but a unity which respects the diversity that enriches us, as is found in any mature family.

The primary aim of all Christians, however, should not be the unity of the Church but the unity of humanity.

Part E: The Church

30 Death

A FAMILIAR, TRADITIONAL UNDERSTANDING

- After death comes the judgement. Then either eternal reward in Heaven or eternal damnation in Hell.

A CONTEMPORARY UNDERSTANDING

- Death is the great unknown.

Talk of death is one of the most unpopular conversation topics. Yet one hundred million of us die each year and it is the one event in human life in which nobody has ever failed!

What happens to us when we die is the great unknown. Theories abound. That after judgement we immediately pass to eternal reward or punishment for our deeds in this life. Or maybe we pass though a period of purification (Purgatory) before enjoying what Christians call the Beatific Vision. Or perhaps it is not so final and that we continue to progress through stages of further spiritual growth. The majority of people in the world believe that we re-incarnate on this Earth and continue through many lives until we have dealt with our karma. Do we ascend to a planet in another galaxy, or even another Universe? In the Hebrew Bible (the Christian's Old Testament) there is no belief in a Beatific Vision. Sheol, the abode of the dead, was the place where the departed were united with their ancestors (Genesis 49:29). In fact, many people believe that our existence ends with death: that there is no "beyond". All is speculation. Nobody knows because nobody has ever come back to tell us.

To that, some might respond: "But Jesus came back to life after his crucifixion". The gospel accounts of the appearances of Jesus after the Resurrection – and they contain many contradictory statements – are not about his being resuscitated to his previous form of life. These are not historical, scientific accounts of a form of life after death but faith witnesses. What we read is that he was recognized by some but not by others. He appeared to those to whom he chose to appear. As we said in Chapter 17, the Greek word translated as "appeared" is *ophthe* which is used for inner spiritual vision rather than for a physical sighting. He never told us about the state of resurrected life he was in. What we would love to know is where, in what state, is Jesus after what is called his Ascension.

The nearest we can get to know about our state after death – and it is not very much – is from the accounts of people who have had a near-death or out-of-the-body experience. What we learn from these is that our consciousness has an existence on its own, outside the physical body, outside the physical brain. There have been recorded cases in which people who had become physically blind had an out-of-the-body experience during a hospital operation. Upon returning to physical consciousness they were able to describe exactly what they had "seen" the surgeon doing to their body, even describing the colours in the operating theatre. All we can say from this is that death could be considered as a transition to another state of consciousness.

Death is an unpopular topic because it brings to our minds the human fear of dying. We are motivated by two primary instincts: the survival instinct and the growth instinct. Death threatens both.

Our fear is not so much a worry about what future state we might be in, as a fear of the process of dying, especially that this might be accompanied by suffering. We fear that final letting-go. We fear entering the unknown, our utter lack of control, our aloneness. Or perhaps the particular image of God that we have causes fear. We have not been helped by images in our minds – and in our classical art – of celestial weighing scales upon the tip of which our eternal destiny depends. Belief in a Last Judgement can cause a deadline anxiety: the fear that there will not be enough time to complete what we think God expects of us.

All our life should be a letting-go process, from ego-centred babyhood unaware of anything other than our needs, through the letting-go of our grown-up children to shape their own lives, to the moment when we have to let go, through dying, of everything upon which we rely for our identity, of everything we depend upon to be in control of our lives.

Sogyal Rinpoche, in his *Tibetan Book of Living and Dying*, suggests that: "Perhaps the deepest reason why we are afraid of death is because we do not know who we are". We rely on props for our identity: names, biography, partners, family, friends, property, professional position, title, bank balance. All these are at the surface level of life, external to us. We would be helped in letting go of our reliance on these props if periodically we were able to escape the constant noise and ceaseless activity that characterize our life in the West. So many people today fear silence, stillness. It reveals their emptiness. We fear to look into ourselves. Meister Eckhart, the medieval mystic, wrote: "Nothing in creation is so like God as stillness".

Those who practise deep, contemplative meditation regularly find they have less fear of dying. This form of prayer enables them to experience that stillness, that silence, to live the present moment, the "now" moment which is the eternal God moment. They become, through this exercise, at ease with passing into an unplotted state of consciousness, of letting go, of letting God take charge.

Appendix

My Creed

I believe in ....

Using this material in groups

The material in this book is suitable for both self-study and as a resource for group discussion. Concepts in the material may be familiar to some people and new to others. Sharing these different understandings enables us to enrich one another and to grow together. The optimum size of a group is between 6 and 12 people.

It is important that all participants be familiar with what is said in the Introduction. The book contains 27 topics, each of which may be used as the basis of a discussion group.

The material may also be adapted to a brief course of five sessions. Such a format may suit a residential week where one session is held on each of five days. Or it may suit a Lent course where one session is held on each of the five weeks in Lent. For a five session course one of the five sections is used for each session. Each section contains between five and seven chapters, and just one chapter is chosen from each part.

If the material is used for a Lent course, for example by local Churches Together, the group leaders should be chosen ahead of time so as to meet together for preparation.

Working in the groups

The following format is suggested for a chapter to be used in a gathering lasting about 1½ hours. Times given are meant to be no more than a guide and may be adjusted according to the judgement of the leader.

Begin with a few moments of attunement:
eg. Be present to (but do not think about) the fact that each of us is a searcher for a deeper understanding of our faith.   3 min.
Someone reads the text aloud – slowly.   10 min.
A time to reflect on it in silence.   5 min.
Without interruption, each person has a turn to share their reflections.   15 min.
A silent time to reflect upon each person's sharing.   5 min.
General, free discussion.   30 min.
A chance to make the sharing our own.
Each one writes down:
– What was new for me in what was shared today?
– What was confirmed by what I heard today?
– Has anything I heard today disturbed me?
– Has anything I heard liberated me today?   5 min.
Share with the others as much or as little as you wish of what you have written down.   10 min.
When everyone has had the chance to speak, end with some moments of attunement:
Just be aware of how much each of us contributes to each other's faith.   3 min.
Agree a date, place and time for the next gathering.

Suggestions for Further Reading

This list of recommended books is provided for those who wish to pursue at a greater depth one or other subject mentioned in these pages.

The books have been chosen on the basis that they are 'easy reading', non-specialist, and that they are up to date: all have been published since 1990.

To obtain an overall picture of the new thinking abroad today, I recommend starting with one or both in the first category and then progress to any of the other subjects which especially appeal to you.

AWAKENING TO A NEW AWARENESS

Diarmuid O Murchu. *Our World in Transition*. Temple House Books, Sussex. 1992. The author, a priest and social psychologist, argues that the coming together in recent years of ecological concerns, scientific exploration, human seeking and spiritual consciousness, is causing us to re-think some of our long-held beliefs and values. Each of his twelve chapters deals with a different factor of life and in each case takes the reader from the traditional understanding to the new perspective.

Lloyd Geering. *The World to Come: from Christian past to Global Future*. Bridget Williams Books Ltd. Wellington, New Zealand. 1999. (Obtainable from Sea of Faith, 15 Burton St, Loughborough, LE11 2DT.)

The author is an Old Testament scholar and Principal of Knox College Theological Hall, Dunedin, New Zealand. The book is divided into two parts: 'The End of the Christian Era' and 'The Beginning of the Global Era'. With a wide-angle lens the author takes us through the various reasons for the present decline in belief that the Christian truths are absolutes, and all the consequences thereof. Globalisation is inevitable and coming fast. While we often hear of its negative effects, Geering sees the positive in the growth of a global consciousness.

DIFFERENT AVENUES TO BE EXPLORED

RELIGION AND SCIENCE

Peter Russell. *The White Hole in Time: Our Future Evolution and the Meaning of Now*. The Aquarian Press (HarperCollins). London. 1992.

One might call this 'A Gospel for the Third Millennium' in that it is the Good News of Liberation in today's language. It is a book of deep spirituality: a call to personal conversion written for the person with a scientific approach to life.

Peter Russell. *From Science to God: The Mystery of Consciousness and the Meaning of Light*. Privately published. 2000. (Available from GreenSpirit, 14 Beckford Close, Warminster. BA12 9LW.)

What is consciousness? This book challenges science's assumption that the "material" is primary reality. He proposes that consciousness is as fundamental as space, time and matter – perhaps even more so. He integrates a deep knowledge of science with his own experience of meditation.

Robert Barry. *A Theory of Almost Everything: A Scientific and Religious Quest for Ultimate Answers*. One World, Oxford. 1993.

Dr. Barry argues that the Grand Unified Theory (that is supposed to explain everything!) will not be found in science alone but in a synthesis of physics, psychology and religion. The Irish News called it: "A major contribution to the debate on who or what we are and where we might be going".

Lloyd Geering (see above). *God and the New Physics*. St Andrew's Trust, New Zealand. 1995. (Obtainable from Sea of Faith, see above) A 50-page "pamphlet", in which very succinctly Geering discusses the religious implications of the contemporary physical sciences.

COSMOLOGY

Brian Swimme & Thomas Berry. *The Universe Story*. HarperCollins. 1994.

These two theologians take us from the Big Bang into this new millennium, tracing the unfolding of the Universe. They suggest the boundless possibilities for our future. The basis of their knowledge is not Revelation but what the Cosmos has to say about itself. It took them ten years to write!

Denis Edwards. *Creation, Humanity, Community: Building a New Theology*. Gill and Macmillan, Dublin. 1992.

In this slim book a Catholic theologian reflects on the challenge to the human community made by our ecological crisis and the advances made by modern science. The work is divided into three main parts and at the end of each are points for further reflection. Edwards provides a theological grounding for Christian involvement in the ecological movement.

Fritjof Capra. *The Web of Life: A New Synthesis of Mind and Matter.* Flamingo (HarperCollins). 1997. Based on ten years of research and discussion with scientists, Capra offers a brilliant synthesis of many of the recent theories of science and on that basis proposes a new foundation for ecological policies that will allow us to build and sustain communities.

D.M.A.Leggett. *Facing the Future: Towards Planetary Welfare.* Pilgrim Books, Norwich. 1990. The planet's future is too important to be left to scientists alone. Leggett, formerly Vice-Chancellor of Surrey University, explores the spiritual implications of today's environmental threats. He bridges the chasm which separates the scientific and religious interpretation of life.

SPIRITUALITY

Bede Griffiths. *A New Vision of Reality: Western Science, Eastern Mysticism and Christian Faith.* Collins. 1989.

This Benedictine monk, writing from his ashram in India, invites us to take a fresh look at Christianity in the context of both modern physics and Eastern mysticism and seeks to demonstrate the basic unity underlying all reality.

William Johnston. *"Arise my Love..": Mysticism for a New Era.* Orbis Books, New York. 2000.

This Irish Jesuit, steeped in Buddhism from his forty years spent in Japan, presents the thesis that the future of Christianity depends upon our moving away from the priority given to doctrine (head stuff) to the experience of the Spirit (heart stuff) particularly through meditation (or, contemplation, as we call this prayer in the West).

Diarmuid O Murchu. *Reclaiming Spirituality.* Gill & Macmillan, Dublin. 1997. The spiritual story of humanity is at least 70,000 years old, whereas formal religion has existed for a mere 4,500 years. The author claims that in many ways religion has subverted spirituality. We need to re-establish its primary significance to give meaning and purpose to human life.

CHRISTIAN BELIEF

Reinhold Bernhardt. *Christianity without Absolutes.* SCM Press. London. 1994. The source of a great deal of conflict in the world is not simply between Religions but because of the absoluteness claimed by these Religions. Reinhold, of the University of Heidelberg, makes the point that Christianity with its absoluteness – held especially by 'fundamentalist' Christians and conservative Catholicism – has much to answer for.

Adrian B. Smith. *The God Shift*. New Millennium. 1996. (Available from the author. 8 Oakthorpe Rd, London N13 5UH) In all aspects of life – scientific, sociological, political, cultural, ethical, psychological – we no longer express ourselves nor understand our world as our parents did. Yet we are expected to believe in and worship a God with concepts that have remained unchanged since the Middle Ages. Hence, Smith claims, there is a sense of unreality today about God, about religion, about the Church.

John Shelby Spong. *Resurrection: Myth or Reality: A Bishop's Search for the Origins of Christianity*. HarperCollins. 1994. This Anglican bishop's challenging writings are known to many Christians. Here is another challenge. Spong argues that because of the strong formative influence of Jewish tradition on the first Christians, most of the details of Jesus' crucifixion and resurrection are not historical. He offers a fascinating and clear suggestion of what really did happen.

THE CHURCH

John Shelby Spong. *Why Christianity must Change or Die*. HarperCollins. 1998. The bishop proposes "a new reformation of the Church's Faith and Practice". He looks ahead to explore the future of ethics, prayer and Christianity itself. He suggests that many Christians today find themselves living in exile similar to the Exile of Jewish history: they feel in exile from the Church in which they were brought up.

Keith Ward. *A Vision to Pursue: Beyond the Crisis in Christianity*. SCM Press, London. 1991. A few of the chapter headings provide the flavour of the book. "The Problem of Saying the Creeds," "Is the Old Testament real History?", "The Uniqueness of Jesus", "Critical Thinking and Religious Authority". Many such contemporary questions are discussed.

John Heaps. *A Love that Dares to Question*. Canterbury Press, Norwich. 2001. An Australian Roman Catholic bishop challenges his Church on a number of contemporary issues that are facing many loyal but wounded Catholics. While the Church is called to be open and reconciling, many are excluded because of its strict ruling on a variety of moral issues.

JESUS THE CHRIST

Albert Nolan. *Jesus before Christianity: The Gospel of Liberation*. Darton, Longman & Todd, London.

The portrait of Jesus that this Dominican priest offers is convincing, challenging and different. He asks: Does Jesus really have anything to say to our troubled world? We are introduced to the Jesus as he was before he became enshrined in doctrines, dogmas and ritual: a man who was deeply involved with the real problems of his time. And how similar they are to our own.

John Dominic Crossan. *Who is Jesus?* HarperCollins. 1996.

This paperback was published to answer the many questions that this Biblical Scholar was asked following his best-selling *The Historical Jesus*. So the matter is presented in question and answer form. In a straight forward way Crossan addresses every subject from Jesus' conception to the miracles, his baptism, his resurrection and more.

John R. Yungblut. *Rediscovering the Christ.* Element Books. 1991. The author, a graduate of Harvard College and Episcopal Divinity School, Cambridge, USA, takes a radical approach to making Jesus come alive again for those who can no longer reconcile the traditional doctrines about Jesus as the Christ with their present world view.

Robert W. Funk. *Honest to Jesus.* HarperCollins. 1996.

This Biblical Scholar, founder of the Jesus Seminar for discerning the authentic words and actions of Jesus, proposes "a Jesus for a New Millennium". He takes the reader through the Gospels and ancient history to find Jesus the subversive, social critic and dissident but also Jesus the sage. Funk proposes a revitalised Christianity, shaped by history, not orthodoxy.

GLOBAL ETHICS AND INTER-FAITH DIALOGUE

Hans Kung. *Global Responsibility: In Search of a New World Ethic.* SCM Press. London. 1990. Kung sets out a programme which he believes it is urgent to pursue if the human race is to survive. He sets it out in three, now widely-quoted, statements. There can be no ongoing human society without a world ethic for the nations. There can be no peace among the nations without peace among the religions. There can be no peace among the religions without dialogue between the religions.

Marcus Braybrooke. *Stepping Stones to a Global Ethic.* SCM Press. London. 1992. The Editor provides a valuable introduction to and copies of 19 declarations and other documents produced as global documents on ethical issues. Starting with the U.N. Declaration of Human Rights in 1948 it goes on to The Earth Charter in 1992. It was intended to show the range of what had already been produced before the 1993 Declaration of the Parliament of the World's Religions but also as a resource for future work. It is still relevant after the 1999 Parliament's

A Call to Our Guiding Institutions which reinforces the need for legislation and action to implement declarations.

Richard Holloway. *Godless Morality: Keeping Religion out of Ethics*. Canongate Books, Edinburgh. 1999. We are all confronted with a moral maze, but the retired Anglican Bishop of Edinburgh proposes that we are not helped in finding our way through it by arguing whether this or that alleged claim for moral truth genuinely emanated from God. Instead, he offers a human-centered justification for a particular moral approach.

Maurice Wiles. *Christian Theology and Inter-religious Dialogue*. SCM Press, London. 1992. Professor Wiles believes that at a time of increasing conservativism and opposition to inter-faith activity in the Churches, a narrow Christianity is not the way forward for our world today. He explains the controversial verse (John 14:6): "No one comes to the Father but by me".

Resources

Further resources are available from:

CANA (Christians Awakening to a New Awareness)
CANA offers people nurture and companionship in their process of awakening and an opportunity to find a commonality with others on a similar spiritual journey.
CANA, 102 Church Road, Steep, Petersfield, GU32 2DD

ONE for Christian Exploration
While supporting those doing Christ's work inside or outside the institutional Church, ONE members explore ways of responding to contemporary Christian issues.
ONE, 34 Stewart Road, London E15 2BB
www.one4god.org

Catholics for a Changing Church
CCC aims to watch and comment on the workings of the Catholic Church, urging it to change internally in its structures and attitudes and in its service to the world, particularly to the poor and oppressed and to God's creation.
CCC, 1 Carysfort House, 14 West Halkin St, London SW1X 8JS

Living Spirituality Network
LSN supports and resources the development of new forms of spirituality both inside and outside the Churches and offers opportunities for people to meet, across all kinds to boundaries.
Living Spirituality Network, The Well at Willen, Newport Rd
Milton Keynes. MK15 9AA

Retreat Association

The Retreat Association puts enquirers in contact with the enormous number and variety of Christian retreats that are available in Britain each year.

Retreat Association, The Central Hall, 256 Bermondsey St London SE1 3UJ

Some recent O Books

The Anglican Quilt

Robert Van de Weyer

This book offers a detailed plan for resolving the present crisis over homosexuality in the Anglican Church, prompted by the appointment of openly gay bishops in the USA and England, and the blessing of a gay partnership in Canada.

Racing the roots of the crisis back to the foundations of Anglicanism over four centuries ago, Robert Van de Weyer shows why ancient divisions have grown wider in recent decades. He argues that the two sides now need separate Episcopal arrangements – yet both sides have much to gain by remaining together in a single body.

A very important contribution. George Carey, former Archbishop of Canterbury

There is much in it to admire…I have no alternative to offer. John Habgood, former Archbishop of York

It should be read by everybody who cares about the future of the Anglican Church. Nicholas Stacey, Clergyman and former deputy director of Oxfam

The author offers solutions that are far preferable to schism and strife. William Frend, retired Professor of Ecclesiastical History at Glasgow University.

I find it both persuasive and stimulating. Anthony Howard, Times columnist and commentator of Church of England affairs

Stimulating, controversial, and full of good sense. Jack Nicholls, Bishop of Sheffield

Robert Van de Weyer is a priest in the Church of England and has ministered in a small village near Cambridge since 1982. He has written over fifty books on theology, world religions, philosophy, church history and economics.

1 903816 89 0
£9.99 $14.95

The Censored Messiah

Peter Cresswell

Peter Cresswell has a revolutionary new theory about the life of Jesus and the origins of Christianity. It is a thrilling story, based on modern scholarship, of how a Jewish man tried to change the direction of the religious leadership of his people. It describes a breathtaking piece of brinkmanship carried out against the Roman occupiers of Israel, a journey into the mouth of death and beyond which appeared to succeed.

Peter Cresswell is a freelance writer with degrees from Cambridge and York Universities in Social Anthropology.

1 903816 67 X
£9.99 $14.95

The Thoughtful Guide to Faith

Tony Windross

This book is for anyone who would like to take faith seriously but finds their intelligence getting in the way. It outlines, in 37 short chapters, many of the objections raised to formal Christian religion, and suggests ways of dealing with them which do not compromise people's intellectual integrity.

The claim made here is that Christianity is far more about the way we live than the way we think, that faith can work for all of us, and that what we may or may not believe must never be allowed to get in the way of faith.

"A *bombe surprise*, unexpectedly lively, adventurous and radical." Don Cupitt, Emmanuel College, Cambridge

Tony Windross is an Anglican minister in Norfolk, England, with degrees from Cambridge University.

1-903816-68-8
£9.99 $14.95

The Thoughtful Guide to the Bible

Roy Robinson

Most Christians are unaware of the revolution in how the Bible may be understood that has taken place over the last two hundred years. This book seeks to share the fruits of the Biblical revolution in an easily accessible manner. It seeks to inform you of its main features and to encourage you to do your own thinking and come to your own conclusions.

Roy Robinson is a United Reformed Church minister, now retired and living in England. A former missionary in Zaire this work arises from a lifetime of study and Bible teaching at the Oxted Christian Centre, which he founded.

1-903816-75-0
£14.99 $19.95

Good As New

A radical re-telling of the Christian Scriptures

John Henson

This radical new translation conveys the early Christian scriptures in the idiom of today. It is "inclusive," following the principles which Jesus adopted in relation to his culture. It is women, gay and sinner friendly. It follows principles of cultural and contextual translation, and returns to the selection of books that the early Church held in highest esteem. It drops Revelation and includes the Gospel of Thomas,

"a presentation of extraordinary power." Rowan Williams, Archbishop of Canterbury

"I can't rate this version of the Christian scriptures highly enough. It is amazingly fresh, imaginative, engaging and bold." Adrian Thatcher, Professor of Applied Theology, College of St Mark and St John, Plymouth

"I found this a literally shocking read. It made me think, it made me laugh, it made me cry, it made me angry and it made me joyful. It made me feel like an early Christian hearing these texts for the first time." Elizabeth Stuart, Professor of Christian Theology, King Alfred's College, Winchester

John Henson, a retired Baptist minister, has co-ordinated this translation over the last 12 years on behalf of *ONE for Christian Exploration*, a network of radical Christians and over twenty organisations in the UK

1-903816-74-2
£19.99 $29.95 hb

Bringing God Back to Earth

John Hunt

Religion is an essential part of our humanity. We all follow some form of religion, in the original meaning of the word. But organised religion establishes definitions, boundaries and hierarchies which the founders would be amazed by. If we could recover the original teachings and live by them, we could change ourselves and the world for the better. We could bring God back to earth.

"The best modern religious book I have read. A masterwork." Robert Van de Weyer, author of *A World Religions Bible*

"Answers all the questions you ever wanted to ask about God and some you never even thought of." Richard Holloway, former Primus Episcopus and author of *Doubts and Loves*

John Hunt runs a publishing company of which O Books is an imprint.

1-903816-81-5
£9.99 $14.95

Tomorrow's Christian

Adrian B. Smith

What are the sources of true Christianity? Tradition or Scripture? Experience? How far should our interpretation accommodate modern knowledge?

Some take refuge in fundamentalism, others in emotion, many are leaving the Church. But there are others, called here "tomorrow's Christian", who struggle to bring together in a meaningful way traditional Christianity and a contemporary, nourishing understanding and expression of it.

36 short chapters sum up the characteristics of tomorrow's Christian. One who is questioning, ecologically aware, global, evolving, non-theistic, balanced, right-brain, scriptural, prophetic, peace-making, forgiving, empowered, Jesus-following, seeking, free, discerning, post-modernist, meditating, mystical and others. Ideal for discussion groups, and all individuals looking outside their churches for a way to live as Christians.

An inspiring and multi-faceted vision of "tomorrow's Christian." The layout with many short chapters makes the book easy to read and digest. I enjoyed reading this book immensely. I find it stimulating and encouraging. Philip Sheppard, *Christians Awakening to a New Awareness*

Adrian B. Smith was ordained as a Roman Catholic priest in 1955.

1 903816 97 1
£9.99/$15.95

O

is a symbol of the world,
of oneness and unity. O Books
explores the many paths of wholeness
and spiritual understanding which
different traditions have developed down
the ages. It aims to bring this knowledge
in accessible form, to a general readership,
providing practical spirituality to today's seekers.

For the full list of over 200 titles covering:

- CHILDREN'S PRAYER, NOVELTY AND GIFT BOOKS
- CHILDREN'S CHRISTIAN AND SPIRITUALITY
- CHRISTMAS AND EASTER
- RELIGION/PHILOSOPHY
- SCHOOL TITLES
- ANGELS/CHANNELLING
- HEALING/MEDITATION
- SELF-HELP/RELATIONSHIPS
- ASTROLOGY/NUMEROLOGY
- SPIRITUAL ENQUIRY
- CHRISTIANITY, EVANGELICAL
AND LIBERAL/RADICAL
- CURRENT AFFAIRS
- HISTORY/BIOGRAPHY
- INSPIRATIONAL/DEVOTIONAL
- WORLD RELIGIONS/INTERFAITH
- BIOGRAPHY AND FICTION
- BIBLE AND REFERENCE
- SCIENCE/PSYCHOLOGY

Please visit our website,
www.O-books.net